IRONCLAD CAPTAINS:

THE COMMANDING OFFICERS OF THE USS *MONITOR*

By

William N. Still, Jr.
Program in Maritime History and Underwater Research
Department of History
East Carolina University
Greenville, NC 27834

Dina B. Hill, Editor

Published by

Marine and Estuarine Management Division
National Oceanic and Atmospheric Administration
United States Department of Commerce

April 1988

For sale by the Superintendent of Documents, U.S. Government Printing Office
Washington, D.C. 20402

I would like to dedicate this volume to Commander John Jannuzzi and Lieutenant Commander Susan Still Jannuzzi, USN.

TABLE OF CONTENTS

List of Figures…………………………………………………………………	ii
Acknowledgements…………………………………………………………	iii
Introduction…………………………………………………………………	1
John Lorimer Worden…………………………………………………………	2
Samuel Dana Greene…………………………………………………………	16
Thomas Oliver Selfridge, Jr.…………………………………………………	23
William Nicholson Jeffers……………………………………………………	36
Thomas Holdup Stevens II.…………………………………………………	49
John Payne Bankhead…………………………………………………………	60
Bibliography…………………………………………………………………	72

LIST OF FIGURES

Figure		Page
1	John Lorimer Worden	2
2	Samuel Dana Greene	15
3	Thomas Oliver Selfridge, Jr.	23
4	William Nicholson Jeffers	35
5	Thomas Holdup Stevens, II	48
6	John Payne Bankhead	59

ACKNOWLEDGEMENTS

I am indebted to many individuals for aid in this work. I especially would like to thank Diana Lange, Edward Miller, Irwin Berent, Charles Perry, Bill Dudley, Dick Von Doenhoff, Pat Gayette, and Fred Ragan. I am most grateful to Dina Hill for her patience and untiring help in the preparation of this manuscript for publication.

INTRODUCTION

The USS *Monitor* is unquestionably one on the best known warships in American history. Virtually every school child has heard of the "*Monitor-Merrimack*" battle in Hampton Roads. Her peculiar "cheesebox-on-a-raft" appearance, with the turret as the prominent feature, is familiar to students of the Civil War and naval history in general. Even her commanding officer during the famous engagement, John L. Worden, is usually recognized by name. But how many are aware that this ironclad vessel-of-war had six commanding officers during her brief existence? Worden was the first, followed by Samuel Dana Greene, Thomas O. Selfridge, Jr., Thomas H. Stevens II, William N. Jeffers, and John P. Bankhead. All were professional naval officers, members of an elite group that Peter Karsten in his book, *The Naval Aristocracy: The Golden Age of Annapolis and the Emergence of Modern American Navalism*, called "Mahan's Messmates," in reference to the fact that they, like the famous naval officer and writer Alfred Thayer Mahan, came of age professionally at a time when the naval officer corps was developing its *espirit de corps*. The Naval Academy, established in 1845, was in its infancy but the "messmates" recognized its enormous value to the profession. The Civil War was The War to many of them, and in fact the majority would never engage in combat again after 1865. They matured during a period of transition in naval warfare, from sail to steam, wood to iron and steel, muzzle-loading smoothbores to breech-loading rifled guns.

The story of each of the six men described in this report stands alone; yet it will also be noted that their paths crossed frequently. One additional point is worthy of emphasis: these officers were together involved in most of the major actions of the Civil War and a large number of minor ones; they saw service in all of the geographical areas and different squadrons; and they participated in nearly every type of activity in which the navy was involved during that five-year period. In short, their combined story constitutes a "case history" of the Union Navy. The six men, although different in age and personality, had one thing in common: they were the only ones to command the *Monitor*.

Figure 1. John Lorimer Worden (Photograph courtesy of the U.S. Naval Historical Center)

JOHN LORIMER WORDEN

John Lorimer Worden was born in Sing Sing (now Ossining), Westchester County, New York, on March 12, 1818, the son of Ananias and Harriet Graham Worden. Ananias Worden was a farmer of modest means. On June 10, 1934, at the age of sixteen, Worden was appointed an acting midshipman in the United States Navy and ten days later was assigned to the eighteen-gun sloop-of-war *Erie*. The *Erie* was under orders to join the Brazil Squadron, and for three years Worden served on this warship in the South Atlantic. On this station young Worden first learned his trade as his vessel provided protection to Americans and their property during a period of revolution and instability in South America. Worden was detached from the *Erie* when she arrived in Boston early in September 1837. After a lengthy period of leave, he returned to Boston and was assigned to the recently launched sloop-of-war *Cyane*. He remained on the *Cyane* for eighteen months before receiving orders to the naval school at Philadelphia, Pennsylvania. Twenty-one-year-old Worden, a veteran of more than four years of active naval service, arrived in Philadelphia two days before Christmas, 1839.

Until after the War of 1812, midshipmen received no formal education beyond that provided by chaplains and schoolmasters on board naval vessels. In 1816 Congress authorized schools at Boston, Norfolk, and Philadelphia which midshipmen could attend voluntarily between voyages. Worden spent seven months at the Philadelphia school, successfully completing the coursework and written examination. On July 15, 1840, he was promoted to passed mishipman.

After leave he was sent to sea on the store ship *Relief*, which was attached to the Pacific Squadron. For nearly three years the *Relief* provided logistical support for units of the Pacific Squadron along the west coasts of North and South America. In 1843 Worden was detached from the store ship. On September 16, 1844, while home on leave, he married Olivia Taffey of Quaker Hill, New York. They would have four children during their long marriage.

On April 7, 1844, Worden was ordered to the Naval Observatory in Washington, D.C., the first of three tours that he served at the observatory. He was one of a number of young officers assigned to this facility, most of them engaged in examining ship's log books and tabulating the results in geographical scales for every month of the year. Although tedious duty, it did allow Worden to be with his wife and during this period the first of their children was born. He purchased a house on K Street, which would be considered home for the remainder of his life.

The year 1846 was a milestone year in Worden's career. He was warrented a master in August and promoted to lieutenant in November. He was then ordered to join the store ship *Southampton* as executive officer.

Worden's promotion and assignment coincided with the first year of the Mexican War. The *Southampton*, under the command of Lieutenant Robert D. Thorburn, was ordered to carry provisions to the units of the Pacific Squadron operating along the coast of California. Arriving on the west coast in the summer, the *Southampton* was used to carry supplies and reinforcements to army and naval units scattered along the coast. When the squadron initiated a blockade along Mexico's coast, the store ship carried provisions and supplies to the blockading vessels. Worden apparently served briefly on other vessels in the Pacific Squadron before being ordered home.

He arrived in New York in the summer of 1849 and, after leave, was assigned to a second tour of duty at the Naval Observatory. Throughout the 1850s he followed the usual ship-to-shore routine, serving on vessels in the Mediterranean and Home squadrons. He

3

served on the frigate *Cumberland* from April 1852 to February 1855; on the sloop-of-war *Levant* for four months; at the Naval Observatory, October 1855 to March 1856; at the Brooklyn Navy Yard until July 1856; and finally as first lieutenant on the frigate *Savannah* until November 1860.

In 1861 Worden was a forty-three-year-old lieutenant, a veteran of twenty-six years of service. His record was satisfactory but certainly not distinguished. Although on active service during the Mexican War, there is no evidence that he saw combat. As has happened many times in history Worden, at that time a middle-aged officer whose career was thus far average, would be catapulted to fame by the chance of war. On the eve of the Civil War Worden, aware that time was passing him by, confided "that the greatest hope of [his] existence" was to become a naval hero.

On April 6, 1861, Worden reported to Washington under orders "for special duty connected with the discipline and efficiency of the naval service." Worden later wrote, "I asked to be relieved from those orders and to be assigned to duty afloat, which was granted." Nonetheless, he did not immediately get the sea duty that was promised: "That night near midnight I was sent for by the Secretary of the Navy who informed me that he wanted me to go at once to Pensacola with dispatches for Captain Henry A. Adams. . .", senior officer commanding the United States Squadron standing off Fort Pickens.

Fort Pickens and Fort Sumter in Charleston harbor were two of the last vestiges of Union authority in the southern states that had seceeded earlier. President Abraham Lincoln was determined to hold on to all Federal property in the southern states that still remained in Union hands, including the two forts. Immediately after Lincoln was inaugurated, reinforcements and supplies were forwarded to the forts.

On the afternoon of April 6, a dispatch arrived from Captain Adams stating that, because of an agreement between the United States government and Confederate authorities, he had declined to obey orders from Secretary of the Navy Gideon Welles to land troops and reinforce Fort Pickens. Welles recorded in his diary that

> [Prompt action] was all important. . . .But, in the general demoralization and suspicion which pervaded Washington, who was to be trusted with this important mission?. . .Paymaster Etting was in Washington, and I sent for him. . .About five o'clock he reported to me that Lieutenant John Worden had just arrived [in the city], that he would vouch for him as untainted by treason.

Welles sent for Worden. He was instructed to carry a message to Captain Adams ordering him to land the troops immediately. Worden was also told to memorize the contents of the message and chew it up and swallow it in the event of capture while en route. He was to leave early in the morning, but in the meantime he was not to mention this assignment to anyone, including his wife.

Early on the morning of April 7, Worden left by train for Richmond and from there for Pensacola. He was stopped several times and in Atlanta had a narrow escape when, as ordered, he destroyed the dispatch just before he was searched. He was not arrested, however, and reached Pensacola on April 10. Before he could obtain transportation out to Adam's flagship under flag of truce, he was taken to the headquarters of General Braxton Bragg, commanding Confederate forces at Pensacola. Worden was given a pass after informing Bragg that he had verbal instructions for Captain Adams. Bragg would later insist that Worden used the words "message of a pacific nature," although Worden's account does not mention this. Worden was also informed that he would be permitted to return to Washington by rail, providing neither Worden nor Adams violated the agreement. On the morning of April 12, Worden reached the flagship and delivered his message to Adams.

Worden returned to Pensacola that afternoon and boarded the first north-bound train. While he was riding northward, Bragg received intelligence that Fort Pickens was to be reinforced. Convinced that Worden's message had led to this action, Bragg ordered his arrest. Worden was apprehended and taken off the train at Montgomery, Alabama, where he was incarcerated in the city jail. He thus became the Confederacy's first prisoner of war.

For seven months--from April 13 to November 13--Worden remained in prison in Montgomery. During this period Mrs. Worden, supported by various naval officers, interceded with Secretary Welles to obtain his release. Unfortunately for Worden, his situation was caught up in the decision by the Lincoln administration to avoid any action that might imply recognition of the Confederacy. Even after the Battle of First Manassas and other engagements in which thousands became prisoners of war, no effort was made to negotiate an exchange of prisoners.

Worden knew little of the efforts on his behalf. Although he was apparently well treated by Confederate authorities, he received few communications from the North. In October, Flag Officer Lewis M. Goldsborough, in command of the North Atlantic Blockading Squadron, proposed to Confederate authorities in Norfolk the exchange of a Confederate naval officer captured at Hatteras for Worden. As a result of these negotiations, Worden left Montgomery on November 13 for Richmond. From there he was taken to Norfolk and, on November 20, the exchange took place under a flag of truce.

Although his health had suffered during the strain of imprisonment, Worden was anxious for active service. On December 3, after a short period of rest and relaxation, he reported to the New York Navy Yard for duty. On January 11, 1862, Commodore Joseph Smith, a member of the "Ironclad Board" established to supervise the Union Navy's armored vessel program and an old family friend, offered Worden the command of the ironclad being built by John Ericsson. "This vessel is an experiment," he said. "I believe you are the right sort of officer to put in command of her." That afternoon Worden hurried to Greenpoint, Long Island, where the vessel was under construction. Convinced that the unusual warship might "prove a success," Worden informed Commodore Smith by return post that he would be willing to "devote whatever capacity and energy I have to that object." His transfer was processed rapidly, and on January 16 he reported for duty to command the new vessel.

Why was Worden, a lieutenant who had never held a command, selected as captain of a warship that was experimental but certainly attractive to more senior officers? It was more than likely a combination of factors. Worden had impressed Navy Department officials, particularly Welles; nearly all officers senior and a number junior to him had already been assigned commands and positions; he was known to Commodore Smith who, as head of the Ironclad Board, was in a position to make the assignment; and finally, he was in the right place at the right time.

At that time Worden was described by one of his officers as

> tall and quite effeminate looking [man], notwithstanding a long beard hanging down his breast--he is white and delicate probably from long confinement and never was a Lady the possessor of a smaller or more delicate hand....He is a perfect gentleman in manner.

It seems likely that Worden's appearance was not normal at this time. He was still recovering from his earlier ordeal and according to Lieutenant Samuel D. Greene, who was appointed the ironclad's executive officer, was "a sick man," who accepted the command "against the protests of his physicians and the entreatment of his family." Nonetheless, he plunged into getting the new vessel launched and operational.

There is nothing unusual in a commanding officer being assigned to a warship still under construction. It provides the captain with time to familiarize himself with his vessel from stem to stern and make any recommendations concerning alterations or modifications that he feels necessary. Although Worden consulted with Ericsson, there are no records concerning any changes that he recommended. Worden also had the responsibility of mounting the ship's ordnance and assembling a crew.

On January 20, four days after Worden assumed command, John Ericsson recommended that the warship be named the *Monitor*. Ten days later, with both Worden and Ericsson on board, the vessel was launched. In the following days, workmen hurried to complete the vessel. On the day after the launching, Worden got the warship's boilers under steam for the first time. With volunteer seamen reporting from the receiving ships, he and his executive officer, Lieutenant Greene, began putting together a watch, quarter and station bill, and assigning the men to their stations. By the middle of February the turret, with its two XI-inch Dahlgren guns, was operational. On February 19 the *Monitor* had her first underweigh trial run. Six days later the vessel was commissioned and the crew officially took over the warship.

Although the *Monitor* was supposed to leave for Hampton Roads on February 27, she was delayed because of mechanical problems. On March 3, under Worden's command, the armored vessel had another trial run to check out her steering qualities and to fire the guns for the first time. Three days later on a clear and cold day, the *Monitor* was towed out of New York City harbor and out into the Atlantic.

The weather deteriorated during the night and, according to the ship's paymaster, Worden was one of many of the crew who became seasick. As the full force of the storm hit, waves began to dash across the ironclad's exposed deck. Water began to seep below in increasing amounts, causing damage to the vessel's blowers and engines and threatening to sink her. Although exhausted from his illness, Worden struggled to keep the vessel afloat. The seas began to moderate early the morning of March 8, and Worden was able to get some rest, leaving the vessel in the capable hands of his executive officer. At noon they passed Cape Charles, at the southernmost tip of the Maryland Peninsula, and entered Chesapeake Bay. During the afternoon as she slowly approached Hampton Roads, still under tow, firing could be heard in the distance. Later when the pilot was taken on board, the crew learned that a small Confederate force, including the ironclad *Virginia*, had attacked Union vessels in Hampton Roads and had done considerable damage.

Worden ordered his ship cleared for action and the turret "keyed" up off the bronze ring, ready to turn. Shortly after dark the *Monitor* slipped her tow, entered the Roads, and by 9:00 P.M. had dropped anchor near the *Roanoke*, which carried the senior officer afloat. Worden went on board the *Roanoke* and conferred with the senior officer. There he learned that the *Monitor* was ordered to the Potomac to defend the river approach to Washington, D.C. The decision was made to ignore the order, and Worden was ordered to defend the *Minnesota*, which had run aground during the day's action with the Confederate vessels. Before returning to the *Monitor*, Worden wrote a hurried note to his wife, informing her of his arrival in Hampton Roads and adding, "the *Merrimac* has caused sad work amongst our vessels, but. . . can't hurt us."

The *Monitor* anchored during the night near the *Minnesota* while the crew got what sleep they could. With daybreak, Worden ordered steam raised and after breakfast was piped down and hastily consumed, the anchor was raised and the *Monitor* steamed slowly along under the towering side of the *Minnesota*. Paymaster Keeler later wrote, "Captain Worden inquired of the *Minnesota* what he intended to do. 'If I can't lighten my ship off I shall destroy her,' Captain Van Brunt replied--'I will stand by you to the last if I can help you,' said our Captain."

As the early morning mist had lifted, the *Monitor*'s crew observed the Confederate ironclad approaching. "A puff of smoke arose from her side and a shell howled over our heads and crashed into the side of the *Minnesota*," Keeler wrote. "Captain Worden, who was on deck, came up and said more sternly than I ever heard him speak before, Gentlemen, that is the Merrimac, you had better go below."

Worden, along with the pilot and quartermaster, crowded into the small pilot house while the executive officer commanded the turret. Worden was supposed to pass his orders to Lieutenant Greene through the speaking tube, but the tube did not work. The paymaster was then used as a messenger between the two officers. Worden ordered the quartermaster to steer directly for the enemy ironclad and once they cleared the *Minnesota*, he sent word to Greene, "Commence firing."

The battle commenced at approximately 8:00 A.M. and ended nearly five hours later. During this long period, the two ironclads pounded each other mercilessly. Throughout most of the encounter, the range was brutally short--less than a hundred yards. Worden hoped to loosen the *Virginia*'s armor by firing at point-blank range, while the Confederate ironclad's captain planned to ram or board his opponent. The *Virginia* was able to ram once, but the *Monitor* turned in time and received only a glancing blow that did no damage except to the *Virginia*, which sprung a leak. The *Monitor* was hit by the Confederate armorclad's heavy guns (twenty-three hits were counted) but with little effect. On one occasion Worden went out on deck to check for damage, and while in this exposed position the *Monitor* was hit. Shortly after this the *Virginia* was able to avoid the *Monitor* briefly and score several hits on the *Minnesota*, but before serious damage could be done the Confederate ship ran aground. As the *Monitor* moved in close to the stranded Confederate warship, a Confederate shell exploded directly outside the pilot house, partially raising its heavy iron cover and driving powder fragments into Worden's eyes and face. Paymaster Keeler wrote,

> I was standing near, waiting for an order, heard the report which was unusually heavy, a flash of light & a cloud of smoke filled the house. I noticed the Capt. stagger & put his hands to his eyes--I ran up to him & asked if he was hurt. 'My eyes,' says he, 'I am blind.' With the assistance of the Surgeon I got him down & called Lieutenant Greene from the turret. A number of us collected around him, the blood was running from his face, which was blackened with the powder smoke. He said, 'Gentlemen, I leave it to you, do what you think best...Save the *Minnesota* if you can.'

Worden was taken to his cabin and placed on the sofa under the care of the surgeon. There he remained until evacuated after the battle was over.

The wounding of Worden may have saved the *Virginia*. The Confederate vessel had run aground and was immobilized when the *Monitor*'s commanding officer was wounded. While he was being attended to, however, the Union warship stood clear of the *Virginia* and during this period the Confederate vessel worked her way clear. Lieutenant Greene decided not to continue the fight but simply to guard the *Minnesota*. Because of some damage, the falling tide, and the belief that the *Monitor* had apparently withdrawn from the engagement, the *Virginia*'s commanding officer made no attempt to renew the fight but withdrew towards Norfolk.

Accompanied by a close friend, Lieutenant Henry A. Wise, Worden was taken ashore and put on the Bay Line steamer for Washington, D.C. In 1888 Worden recalled the help that Wise rendered him in a letter to Wise's daughter:

> To his friendly care and attention in bringing me
> from Hampton Roads after my injuries in the
> *Monitor* and putting me in his own bed at his home

> in Washington, and the devoted care and attention given to me there, for several weeks by himself and his wife, I am largely indebted for my recovery from the injuries I received, and their resulting complications.

Worden had been seriously wounded and spent more than eleven weeks recovering. According to a statement accompanying a petition for a pension for Mrs. Worden after her husband died,

> ...the injury was produced in a great measure from unburned powder, minute portions of iron from the broken bar of the pilot house being driven into the texture about his eyes. The powder and iron were driven in great quantities into the texture about the lids and the integumen over the temples. Tumefaction was very great, as likewise the pain, so that no thorough attempt was made to remove some portions of the powder and iron that were embedded in the tissues.

Worden's face was permanently blackened and the sight in his left eye was destroyed.

Worden never completely recovered his health. "My head was all knocked to pieces at Hampton Roads," Worden later said. "For three months, I lay unconscious and when I woke to life again, I was a mental wreck. Since then I have never known the time when I wasn't suffering both physical and mental pain." He said this in 1895, two years before his death.

During the latter part of May 1862, he was able to return to his summer home in New York. There he consulted an occulist and his eyesight greatly improved.

While recovering Worden was lauded for the battle. Messages of praise, congratulations, and sympathy showered upon him during his months of convalescence. In Washington President Lincoln visited him and thanked him for his efforts to save the country. The state of New York presented him with a sword and testimonial. Twice, on July 11, 1862, and February 3, 1863, he received the thanks of Congress for "skill and gallantry." In July he was promoted to commander.

Not all joined in the adulation. Some naval officers questioned the praise lavished on him, stressing that although Worden had commanded his ship ably until incapacitated by his wound, that was no more than what any commanding officer of a warship should have done. Flag Officer Samuel DuPont wrote his wife on May 13, 1862, "I saw in the last paper that Lieutenant Worden had gone to the Senate Chamber with a handkerchief round his head and was Lionized--this pained me much and shows he is a weak man, I don't care how brave." Flag Officer Charles H. Davis wrote that Commander John Rodgers

> called my attention to the difference between the praises and honors awarded to Worden and the neglect shown to [Lieutenant George] Morris [commanded the *Cumberland*], although the latter's courage and patriotism were put to the severest test. He fought his guns while his ship was sinking, and cheered as she was going down. Such are the charm of novelty and success.

John Ericsson, in a speech before the New York Chamber of Commerce, lauded Chief Engineer Alban C. Stimers, who was on board the *Monitor* as a volunteer and assisted Lieutenant Greene in the turret. Ericsson said that the success of the *Monitor* was due "entirely. . .to the presence of. . .Stimers." Although Worden protested in a letter to Ericsson when he heard of this remark, Ericsson reiterated this on several occasions.

On May 8, one day less than two months since he was wounded, Worden received orders to the ironclad *New Ironsides* under construction in Philadelphia. He apparently never joined the vessel and was detached shortly before she was commissioned. He was then ordered to New York to assist in the construction of ironclads at the Navy Yard. There is little question that he was detached from the *New Ironsides* and ordered to shore duty in New York because he had not recovered sufficiently for an active sea command.

Apparently he had recovered by the end of the year, at least to the satisfaction of the Navy Department, because on October 8 he was ordered to take command of the *Montauk*, a new and improved single-turreted monitor built by Ericsson at the Continental Iron Works in Greenpoint. The following day the new warship was launched. It was commissioned on December 14. On Christmas Eve, the *Montauk* departed New York for duty with the South Atlantic Blockading Squadron and arrived at Port Royal, South Carolina, in the middle of January 1863.

Worden would see considerable action during the six months that he commanded the *Montauk*. Shortly after she arrived at Port Royal, Flag Officer DuPont, in command of the South Atlantic Blockading Squadron, ordered Worden to Ossabow Sounds, Georgia. DuPont wanted to test the new monitor type against land fortifications and instructed the *Montauk*'s commander to attack Fort McAllister, about ten miles up the Great Ogeechee River. Another objective was the destruction of the Confederate raider *Nashville*, which was lying under the guns of the fort waiting for an opportunity to slip through the Union blockade.

On January 27, Worden attacked the fort. His volunteer signal officer wrote,

> It was a dull morning and too early for anybody to feel hungary [sic]. Besides most of the *Montauk*'s crew had never been under fire. . . .We started up the river at five minutes of seven. . . .It was ebb tide and we steamed up grandly. All at once we passed a clump of trees, and the fort was in plain view. . . . No sign of life appeared in the fort as we approached--not even a flag. . . .At 7:30 we were within fifteen hundred yards of the fort, and let go anchor. Five minutes later, at the word of command, the turret beneath us began slowly to revolve. A few moments and the big eleven-inch gun was at range, elevated for fifteen hundred yards. 'Stop!' and the turret came to a standstill. 'Fire!' and for an instant one's heart stood still, waiting. Then the floor of the pilot-house lifted and heaved and shook with the mighty roar of the gun a few inches beneath, and a moment later a great shell exploded just short of the enemy's work.
>
> But. . .we discovered that the fortress was not abandoned. At 7:40 precisely there came a flash from up there and a well-aimed ten-inch shot struck us on the gunwale, raising a ruffled edge on one of the plates, but doing no damage. . . .We now loaded and fired as fast as possible. . . .Above and about us shells exploded, rattling against our armour, making

an infornal raket [sic], but doing little or no harm. The smoke got very thick about the pilot-house, blowing in at the peep holes, and annoying Worden so that presently he went below to inspect the working of the turret and to note the effect of the heavy guns upon the vessel. . . .We now realized that we had underestimated our enemy. Our ammunition was running low, and while we had pounded the works severly [sic] and made a good deal of sand fly, we had apparently done little harm . . .at noon when our last shells were nearly gone we weighed anchor and dropped down the stream. . . An hour later we were at our anchorage, counting our scars.

Five days later the fort was attacked again. During the second attack Worden anchored his vessel 150 yards from the obstructions that guarded the fort and once again opened a deliberate fire, but with the same results. As B. S. Osbon, the signal officer, wrote, "Our battle of February 1st was a repetition of our former action, much intensified." During this engagement forty-six shells struck the monitor without doing any damage. DuPont later wrote,

I sent him [Worden] with his ironclad to see what he could do--mainly to test in <u>earnest</u> the power and capabilities of his vessel. . . .He made the attack, fired away all his ammunition and made but little impression. . . Still we gained a great deal of information as to the management of those vessels.

Two days after the attack Worden was promoted to captain.

During the evening of February 27, the *Nashville* was observed to be underway above the fort. Within a short period, however, it was observed that she had run aground. At daylight the following morning, the *Montauk* moved up to approximately 800 yards from the fort and opened fire on the still-grounded Confederate vessel. The *Nashville* was visible behind the fort where the river made a sharp bend. Osbon, who was in the pilot house with Worden during the engagement with the *Nashville*, wrote,

At seven minutes past seven o'clock we fired our first shot. . .at the Nashville. . .the smoke from our gun rises slowly, and we cannot see the effect of the shell. . .From the fort they are firing [at us]. But we pay no attention to the fort, not returning any of its fire. Again we send a shell where the smoke hides her from us. The fifth shot, that entered near the foremast, has done its work, and we can see a column of whitish-gray smoke issuing from her fore-hatch, and in five minutes more tongues of flame leap out with the smoke, high into the air. . . .We fire our last shot at three minutes after eight o'clock, having fired fourteen times.

When the smoke lifted the *Nashville* was discovered to be in flames and approximately an hour later her magazine exploded.

The monitor, undamaged from the fort's fire, began to withdraw down river, but a torpedo exploded under the hull and she started taking on water. "Captain Worden turned to the pilot and said to him, 'Murphy, can't you run me ashore here in some good place?' " The *Montauk* was run ashore, a piece of boiler iron fastened over the hole, and she resumed steaming down the river.

DuPont wrote that "Worden was so worried at the idea of his vessel being injured that. . .he could not enjoy his success," and added, "Everyone says what a lucky man Worden is--that is true in one sense, but it is not everyone who would have gone right up under the fort again." This from a naval officer who was somewhat critical of Worden's actions after the *Monitor-Virginia* affair. D. Ammens, in *The Atlantic Coast*, wrote that in later years Worden was prouder of the destruction of the *Nashville* than of the battle with the *Virginia*.

Within two weeks of destroying the *Nashville*, the *Montauk* was moored in the North Edisto River near Charleston along with six other armorclads including the *New Ironsides* and the *Keokuk*. The Navy Department had instructed DuPont to attack the forts guarding the entrance to Charleston harbor, and the flag officer decided to make the attack with all of his ironclads. At noon on April 7, the nine armored vessels stood up the channel in single line ahead with the *Weehawken* leading, followed by the *Passaic* and the *Montauk*. The *Montauk* came into action at 3:05 P.M., firing her XI-inch and XV-inch Dahlgrens at Fort Sumter. At 4:30 DuPont ordered the vessels to disengage and withdraw; the attack had failed. During the engagement the *Montauk* had fired only twenty-seven times and in turn had been hit fourteen times but with no material damage. The nine ironclads together delivered only 139 rounds during the approximately one-hour-and-forty-minute-battle.

Worden's futile attacks on Fort McAllister had demonstrated to DuPont that monitors were not suitable as offensive vessels to attack strong land fortifications. The April 7 bombardment was made despite the flag officer's reservations, and he strongly disapproved of it to the Department. He wrote Secretary Welles,

> I remind the Department that ability to endure is not sufficient element where-with to gain victories, that endurance must be accompanied with a corresponding power to inflict injury upon the enemy. . .that the weakness of the monitor class of vessels. . .is fatal to their attempts against fortifications.

Worden agreed and later strongly denounced monitors in assaults against forts before a court of inquiry.

The April 7 battle was Worden's last, not only for the war but for the remainder of his career. DuPont wrote his wife,

> Poor Worden will return home; his nervous system is shatered [sic]. . .He has struck me with intense admiration since he has been here, and when I told him he should go in time and pleasure and that no medical survey was necessary, and that I felt proud at having had him under my command, he wept like a child.

Worden returned to New York where he was once again given responsibilities concerning the construction of ironclads in the city. As before, he was apparently placed on a kind of limited-duty status in order to regain his health. He was still in this position when the Civil War ended, and in fact retained it until February 1866. In August he was assigned to command the steamer *Pensacola* in the North Pacific Squadron but was relieved in May 1867. For the next two years he was at home "awaiting orders," except for a brief period of "special duty." For six months of this period he visited Europe. On May 27, 1868, he was promoted to commodore.

On December 1, 1869, he was ordered to the Naval Academy as superintendent. Worden's tenure at the Academy was not particularly impressive, at least in part because he made no secret of his belief that midshipmen would benefit more from being on board warships than at Annapolis. Lieutenant George Dewey, later admiral, was aide to Worden. In his autobiography Dewey described one incident that illustrated Worden's "Old Navy" perspective:

> He had a midshipman up for some infraction of discipline, and he broke out: 'Where you ought to be, young man, is not ashore in a landsman's school, but on board a ship, where you would learn the business of being a seaman in the same hard school that I learned it.'
> At this, well knowing the admiral's views on the score, which were often repeated, the midshipman grinned slightly, perhaps unconsciously. 'Don't you grin at me or I will throw you out of the window!' Worden blazed. The midshipman's face went very stiff and sober at such a 'dressing down' from the autocrat of Annapolis and one of the great heroes of the war. For some reason I myself could not resist a smile at the situation, and the admiral caught me at it, too. For a minute I did not know but he might try to throw me out of the window. However, he controlled his temper and said nothing.

There is also a story in Dorothy Michelson Livingston's biography of her father, Albert Michelson, in which Worden chides the future Nobel Laureate: "If in the future you'd give less attention to those scientific things and more to your naval gunnnery, there might come a time when you would know enough to be of some service to your country."

One history of the Naval Academy said, "Worden was not an innovator . . . .No doubt he would have been entirely at a loss if anybody had suggested that he should embark upon any radical reforms." He made no noticeable changes in the Academy's curriculum or organization and very little so far as the grounds and facilities were concerned.

His administration was most noted because of difficulties over hazing plebes by upperclassmen and the admission of the Academy's first minority midshipman. Several Japanese were enrolled and in 1872 the first Black midshipman was appointed by a Reconstruction congressman from South Carolina. Although most of the officers and faculty apparently were not quite ready for emancipation, they did everything they could to prevent problems. Two more Blacks were appointed during Worden's time at the Academy but none graduated.

In early 1874 Captain C. R. P. Rodgers, Worden's successor at the Academy, wrote the Secretary of the Navy:

> The admirable condition and very high state of efficiency in which the Naval Academy was left, by my predecessor, Rear Admiral J. L. Worden, left me little to do, but to continue the routine of his administration and follow in his steps. I feel under

great obligation to him for the care he has taken to
make my succession easy and agreeable.

In September 1872, Worden was relieved as superintendent, and on November 20, promoted to rear admiral. Three months later Worden was ordered to assume command of the European Squadron.

The European Squadron was activated towards the end of the Civil War in order to seek out and destroy Confederate cruisers in European waters. The squadron's peacetime mission evolved around supporting American diplomatic, commercial, and military interests abroad. Support was at times simply showing the flag; at other times, it involved a demonstration, intervention, "police action," or what became known as "gunboat" or "battleship" diplomacy.

The parsimonious nature of Congress in the post-war years so far as the military was concerned affected Worden's squadron. His force was gradually reduced until, by the fall of 1876, it consisted of one third-rate wooden sloop-of-war, the *Marion*. A distressed Worden wrote the Navy Department that "for two weeks the *Marion* was in the yard, and there were no American warships to protect American interests." This situation changed, however, because of trouble in the Ottoman Empire.

In the spring of 1876 an insurrection broke out in some of the Ottoman possessions in the Balkans. In the months that followed the disorders spread into other parts of the Empire, including Constantinople. The American minister to Turkey appealed to the State Department for naval protection. Worden took advantage of the crisis to urge reinforcing his squadron. The appeal did little good, however. He was able to send only two vessels, the *Franklin* and the *Marion*, to the eastern Mediterranean. Worden took the *Marion* to Constantinople to help guard American interests there.

In October the crisis deepened with the imminent possibility of war between Russia and Turkey. Once again Worden pleaded for more ships. The Department promised him two additional vessels, the *Vandalia* and *Trenton*. The *Vandalia* arrived at the end of November, but the *Trenton* did not arrive until the following March. Before they arrived, however, Worden's predicament became ludicrous. At one point, while the *Marion* was undergoing repairs in a French shipyard, he had hoisted his flag on a hotel in Nice. It became something of a joke to the French, who referred to it as "l'amiral Suisse."

On April 24, 1877, Russia declared war on Turkey. Under orders from Washington, Worden concentrated the entire European Squadron in Turkish waters. The *Vandalia* was sent to Constantinople, the *Marion* and *Trenton* to Smyrna, and a recently arrived fourth vessel, the *Alliance*, was stationed off the Syrian coast. Throughout the summer and early fall months, the squadron remained in Turkish waters. The vessels were still there in October when Rear Admiral William E. LeRoy relieved Worden.

The European Squadron was Worden's last active comand. In the last years of his career, he served as president of both the Naval Retiring Board and Examining Board. In December 1886, he voluntarily retired after fifty-two years in the navy. According to a letter that he wrote to a newspaper reporter in March of that year, his health was not good. In fact, during the last years of service he was hospitalized on six different occasions for various illnesses.

Although he would live nearly nine years after retiring, the few surviving pieces of correspondence suggest that he remained in poor health. We know very little about these years. He lived in Washington, D.C., but spent his summers at Quaker Hill, New York. One of Worden's neighbors and friends at Quaker Hill was General Lew Wallace, the author of *Ben Hur*. Wallace and Worden frequently took walks together. In Washington, Worden served as president and governor of the Washington Metropolitan Club, and according to one account was one of the "best known and most popular residents of the nation's capital."

Rear Admiral Worden died suddenly of pneumonia on Monday, October 18, 1897, at his K Street home in Washington. He was eighty years old at the time of his death. A state funeral was held for him at Saint John's Episcopal Church on October 20 with President McKinley, members of the cabinet, and a large number of naval officers present. He was buried in Pawling, New York.

Worden was not a brilliant officer, but a brave and competent one. He was greatly respected by his fellow officers. In 1891 Captain C. R. P. Rodgers wrote another officer concerning a campaign to erect a statue to Admiral David D. Porter at the Naval Academy: "I should like to see such a statue to Porter, placed at Annapolis, and later one to Worden."

Figure 2. Samuel Dana Greene (Photograph courtesy of U.S. Naval Historical Center).

SAMUEL DANA GREENE

Samuel Dana Greene was born on February 1, 1840, in Cumberland, Maryland, of New England parentage. His father was George Sears Greene of Rhode Island, a regular army officer who was promoted to brigadier general two months after the *Monitor-Virginia* battle. On September 21, 1855, Samuel entered the navy as an "acting midshipman" on probation at the Naval Academy at Annapolis.

One of his classmates was Alfred T. Mahan, who occasionally remarked on midshipman Greene in letters to friends. In one letter Mahan mentioned that Greene had been caught by the officer of the day after a prank, and in another he was critical of Greene's actions while both were on their way to New York for the holidays. Referring to this incident Mahan wrote, "It takes at least twenty gentlemen to remove the bad impression made by one rowdy." With the exception of this lone criticism, Mahan's impressions suggest that Greene was a typical midshipman, studious when necessary, but quite willing to challenge the Academy's sense of propriety at times. He apparently never got into serious trouble and graduated in 1859, seventh in a class of twenty.

Promoted to midshipman, he was ordered to the *Hartford* upon graduation. Greene was apparently a plank owner on the *Hartford*, which was commissioned in May 1859 at the Boston Navy Yard where Greene reported on board. The *Hartford* was a steam sloop-of-war carrying twenty-four guns. She was ordered to join the East India Squadron as the flagship of Commodore Cornelius K. Stribling. In November 1859, she embarked the American minister to China, John Elliott Ward, at Hong Kong and carried him to Canton, Manila, Swatow, Shanghai, and other Far Eastern ports to settle American claims and to arrange for favorable consideration of the nation's interests. Her presence as a symbol of American sea power materially contributed to the success of Ward's diplomatic mission. We know nothing of Midshipman Greene's life during these months in the Far East, but he must have had a successful cruise as he was promoted to lieutenant before returning home.

With the outbreak of the Civil War the *Hartford*, along with most of the other warships on distant station, was ordered home. She arrived in Philadelphia on December 2, 1861, nearly nine months after the firing on Fort Sumter. There Lieutenant Greene was detached and after a brief leave, volunteered for service on the *Monitor*. The shortage of junior officers in the navy is the probable explantation for the fact that Greene, at twenty years old, was appointed executive officer of the vessel. The paymaster described the newly appointed executive officer as "a young man. . .in regular service, black hair and eyes that looked through a person and will carry out. . .orders." In contrast to Captain Worden, Greene was clean-shaven and his youthfulness did not retard the crew's respect for him. A crew member of the *Florida*, where Greene would later be executive officer, mentioned in his diary that Greene seemed "to be a very good sort." Apparently, Worden and his new executive officer worked well together, as Worden always spoke very highly of him.

Greene assisted Worden in preparing the *Monitor* for sea. It was Greene, as executive officer, who had the responsibility for assigning crew members to their watches and quarters. He was also gunnery officer and began training the crew at the two Dahlgrens in the turret.

Under tow of the tug *Seth Low*, the *Monitor* departed New York on March 6, 1862. Within twenty-four hours the vessels ran into heavy weather as they plotted their way southward towards Hampton Roads. Worden, obviously still weak from his months of being a prisoner of war, became seasick. As the storm increased, the *Monitor* began to take on water. The water coming down the blower vents resulted in the breaking of a fan, which put the blowers out of service. Carbon dioxide spread from the engine room up to the berth deck, forcing the crew to abandon those spaces. Greene hurried below to make sure no one was left. "I was nearly suffocated with the gas myself, but got on deck...just in time...." Greene later wrote. Efforts to pump out the water failed and for a while it looked as if the *Monitor* might sink. Fortunately, the tug was able to pull the foundering ironclad in closer to land where the water was considerably calmer. The gas was then cleared out. The engineer repaired the blower and restarted the engines and pump.

Worden was still ill, so Greene volunteered to take the watch. Near midnight the weather had calmed to the point that Greene also retired. Within a brief period, however, the waves picked up, again flooding the vessel. About 3:00 A.M. the weather moderated once again, but with Worden still incapacitated, a nervous Greene remained on watch. The period from then until dawn was, Greene said, "...the longest hour and a half I ever spent."

During the following day, March 8, the vessel was cleaned, repairs made, and normal routine re-established. At noon the vessels entered the Chesapeake Bay and by early afternoon they had passed Cape Henry and were approaching Hampton Roads.

We know little of Greene's activities from the time firing was heard in the distance to the following morning when the battle with the *Virginia* commenced. We can assume that he had his responsibilities as executive officer in preparing the vessel for combat. Greene does mention that he and Worden remained on deck throughout the night. "At 11 P.M.," Greene wrote, "I went on board [the stranded *Minnesota*]...and asked the Captain what his prospects were of getting off. He said he should try to get afloat at 2 A.M. when it was high water....I told him we should do all in our power to protect him from the attack of the *Merrimac*."

The following morning the Confederate vessels, including the *Virginia*, made their appearance, steaming towards the stranded *Minnesota*. Worden took his station in the pilot house and Greene took command of the turret. When firing was heard in the distance, Greene sent paymaster Keeler to the pilot house for permission to open fire. (The speaking tube that connected the turret with the pilot house was not working). Worden replied, "Tell Mr. Green [sic] not to fire till I give the word...." Shortly afterwards, Greene was ordered to "commense [sic] firing." It was approximately 8:45 A.M. when Greene fired the first shot at the approaching Confederate armorclad. Throughout the morning hours, the two ironclads slugged it out at ranges from more than a hundred yards to at times almost touching. Greene wrote his parents,

> I had not slept a wink for 51 hours. But after the first gun was fired [I]...forgot all fatigue, hard work and everything else.... We loaded and fired as fast as we could. I pointed and fired the gun myself. Every shot I would ask the Captain the effect, and the majority of them were encouraging.

Both vessels bounced shot and shell off each other's sides with little effect. The fact that the *Virginia* would escape with little apparent damage led later to criticism of Greene's gunnery. In his report, Worden praised Greene's gunnery and years after the war, in a letter to a reporter, wrote that "claims of Lieutenant Greene's poor gunnery is all bosh." His gunnery was accurate; his guns simply could not penetrate the *Virginia*'s armor.

When Worden was wounded by a shell striking the pilot house, Greene was ordered to take charge of the vessel and to "use [his] own discretion." The *Monitor* had withdrawn from the action after Worden was wounded, and during the approximately half-hour period before Greene assumed command, the two protagonists drifted apart. Shortly after Greene took over, the *Virginia* was observed apparently retiring in the direction of Norfolk. The *Virginia*'s commanding officer later wrote that when the *Monitor* retired into shoal water (when Worden was wounded), he assumed that the *Monitor* had broken off the engagement. By this time the *Monitor* was approximately a mile from the Confederate ironclad and Greene turned his vessel towards the *Minnesota*. "We had strict orders, Greene later wrote, "to act on the defensive, and protect the *Minnesota*." Greene did not pursue the *Virginia* for this reason and also because of Worden's wound and the need to get him more medical assistance. Finally, he considered the *Virginia*'s movement towards Norfolk an indication that the Confederate ironclad was beaten.

After anchoring near the *Minnesota*, Worden was evacuated and the ship secured from combat conditions. Later in the evening Gustavus Fox, the Assistant Secretary of the Navy, came on board and said, "Well, gentlemen. . .you don't look as though you were just through one of the greatest naval conflicts on record." "No sir," replied Lieutenant Greene. "We haven't done much fighting, merely drilling the men at the guns a little." Despite the executive officer's flippant remark, there is little doubt that Greene, as well as his inexperienced crew, had been under enormous tension throughout the day. Greene told his parents that

> I had been up so long, had had so little rest, and been under such a state of excitement, that my nervous system was completely run down. Every bone in my body ached, my limbs and joints were so sore that I could not stand. My nerves and muscles twitched as though electric shocks were continually passing through them. . .I laid down and tried to sleep, but I might as well have tried to fly.
>
> The next morning we got under weigh at 8 o'clock and stood through our fleet. Cheer after cheer went up from frigates and small craft for the glorious little *Monitor*. . . .I was Captain then of the vessel that had saved Newport News, Hampden [sic] Roads, Fortress Monroe. . .and perhaps four Northern ports.

Greene's exaggerated sense of accomplishment and self-adulation is understandable. He was a very young officer who, through fortuitous circumstances, had found himself in command of a warship that, even to those present at the time, realized its historic importance. Also, Federal leaders from President Lincoln down had been convinced that the *Virginia* was a threat to Washington, New York City, and other cities along the eastern seaboard.

Greene's exhilaration as captain was all too brief. On the afternoon of March 10, Greene received a note from Assistant Secretary of the Navy Fox informing him that Lieutenant Thomas O. Selfridge, Jr., had been appointed temporary commander. "Of course I was a little taken about," a disappointed Greene wrote, for he apparently hoped that he would receive command. He told his parents, "Between you and me I would have kept the command with all its responsibilities and either the Merrimac or the Monitor should have gone down in our new engagement. But you know all young people are vain, conceited and without judgement."

Greene returned to the unrecognized and unrewarded (as far as the public was concerned) responsibility of executive officer and remained in this position until the *Monitor* went down off Cape Hatteras. He would serve under four commanding officers during this ten-month period.

The *Monitor* would remain in Hampton Roads until the *Virginia* was destroyed by her own crew. Early in June the *Monitor* sortied up the James River and, along with other Union warships, engaged Confederate batteries at Drewry's Bluff. Afterwards she would operate in the James and Appomattox rivers, occasionally exchanging fire with

Confederates, interspersed with trips back to Hampton Roads. In September she was ordered to the Washington Navy Yard for alterations and overhaul before returning to Hampton Roads two months later.

Throughout this period, Greene's name was never mentioned in the occasional reports or pieces of correspondence from the *Monitor's* commanding officer. We know nothing about him during these months except for one incident mentioned in a letter from the ship's paymaster to his wife. In the latter part of June, the *Monitor* accompanied a small Union flotilla up the Appomattox River to destroy a railroad bridge. Because of the shallowness of the river near the bridge, the attack was to be made by a number of small boats. Greene was in charge of one of these small boats. The attack, however, failed and the vessels returned back downstream with the bridge still intact.

In December the *Monitor* was ordered to join a blockading squadron further south, and on December 29 departed Hampton Roads under tow of the steamer *Rhode Island*. During this last voyage of the *Monitor*, Greene again acted creditably and courageously, particularly during the ship's final hours. When the ship was finally abandoned, Greene took charge of evacuating the crew into the small boats sent by the *Rhode Island*. As the *Monitor* pitched and rolled in the mountainous waves, Greene struggled to get the men into the boats. The ship's surgeon, Greenville Weeks, wrote,

> Greene nobly held his post, seized the rope from the whaleboat, wound it about an iron stanchion, and then around his wrists, for days afterwards swollen and useless from the strain. His body servant stood near him,
> 'Can you swin, William?' he asked.
> 'No,' replied the man.
> 'Then keep by me, and I'll save you.'

The captain and Greene were the last in the boat, which then returned to the *Rhode Island*. The *Monitor's* commanding officer, John P. Bankhead, in his official report of the vessel's loss, wrote,

> I would beg leave to call the attention of the Admiral and of the Department of the particularly good conduct of Lieutenant Greene and Acting Master [Louis] N. Stodder, who remained with me until the last, and by their example did much toward inspiring confidence and obedience on the part of the others.

In February 1863, Commander Bankhead was ordered as captain of the USS *Florida*, a side-wheel steamer purchased by the government and converted into a naval vessel for blockade duty. At Bankhead's request, Greene was assigned as executive officer. On March 9 the *Florida*, with the new monitor *Nantucket* in tow, left the New York City Navy Yard to join the North Atlantic Blockading Squadron. She joined the squadron early in April, and for the next twenty-one months patrolled the North Carolina coast, capturing a steamer and a number of blockade runners.

We know very little about Greene during this period. The letters of Paymaster Keeler, also aboard the *Florida*, to his wife occasionally mention Greene such as when he drilled the gun crews or took possession of one of the prizes. Early in August 1863, Commander Bankhead became ill and had to be sent north for treatment. Once again Greene was a temporary commanding officer until another one was assigned. During the night of August 15, the *Florida*, under Greene's command, gave chase to a blockade runner near Wilmington but without success. Two days later he had another opportunity.

> On Monday, the 17th, at about 7 p.m., discovered a strange sail standing directly up for the squadron. From our masthead made her out to be a small side-wheel, beam-engine steamer, painted white; ordered the *Victoria* to go out and see what she was. As soon as the *Victoria* started for her the strange sail altered her course more to the westward....As this vessel was about underway and standing down for the stranger, discovered another vessel bearing E. and apparently a very short distance from us. This second vessel appeared to have a light illuminating her bow, but as soon as I started for him he extinguished his light, and it being very dark, nothing more was seen of him. . . .I now stood down in the direction of the dim light showing from the strange sail, bearing about W.S.W. The *Victoria* made the Coston [sic] signal O, and I answered with the same, when the stranger immediately put out his light and nothing more was seen of him....Nothing was in sight up the river in the morning, and I do not think either vessel went in.

This was Greene's last opportunity. A week after the futile chase, a new commanding officer, Lieutenant Commander James Parker, reported on board and Greene resumed his executive officer status. Because of ill health Parker left within a few weeks, and Lieutenant Commander Walter W. Queen took command. Within a few days, Greene himself left the *Florida*. His reason for being detached was to get married. However, one wonders if the posting of two commanding officers over him was not a factor. He left the ship on September 20, and on October 9 he was married to Mary Willis Dearth of Bristol, Rhode Island. They would have three children before she died unexpectedly in 1874.

In November Paymaster Keeler, still on the *Florida*, mentioned to his wife that he had received a letter from Greene informing him that

> He has been ordered on 'shore duty' at the New York Navy Yard, as a sort of Assistant Inspector of purchased vessels and is associated with Capts. Worden and Bankhead....Mr. Greene wrote in fine spirits and said he had sent the messa box of his wedding cake but it has failed to reach us.

Greene's shore duty was short-lived. On December 16, Keeler wrote that Greene had been ordered to the *Iroquois* and added, "I hoped that his marriage would induce him to quit drinking but I fear it has not."

There is no evidence other than Keeler's remark to suggest that Greene drank excessively. Heavy drinking was not that uncommon among naval officers during the Civil War. Keeler may well have been simply voicing his disapproval of drinking, entirely. In fact, he mentions that another one of the *Monitor*'s commanding officers was a heavy drinker.

The commanding officer of the *Iroquois* was Commander Christopher Raymond Perry "Alphabet" Rodgers, one of the most liked officers in the naval service. Greene presumably got along well enough with Rodgers for he remained executive officer of the *Iroquois* until the war was over. The *Iroquois* was a steam sloop-of-war which carried a battery of six guns. Under Rodgers' command, the warship served briefly in the North

Atlantic Blockading Squadron before being ordered to European waters. During the fall of 1864 and the winter of 1865, she remained stationed off Bordeaux, France, where several armored vessels were supposedly being built for the Confederacy. She then joined in the world-wide search for the Confederate raider *Shenandoah*. This search took the *Iroquois* around South America and across the Pacific, arriving in Singapore in May 1865. With the war over, she sailed in July for the United States, arriving in New York on October 1, 1865.

Greene was immediately detached from the *Iroquois* and ordered to report to the Naval Academy as an instructor. He was also informed that, as of August 11, he had been promoted to lieutenant commander. For more than half of the period between 1866 and 1884, he was attached to the Naval Academy, serving at different times as instructor in mathematics; head of the Department of Astronomy, Navigation, and Surveying; assistant in charge of buildings and grounds; and aide to the superintendent.

In 1868 Greene was ordered to the North Pacific Squadron with headquarters in San Francisco. For a brief period, he commanded the ill-fated, paddle-wheel gunboat *Seginaw*, which struck a reef and wrecked a few months after he left the ship. In 1872 he was promoted to commander. Between 1875 and 1877 he commanded the steam sloop-of-war *Juniata* and the training ship *Monongahela*.

When Greene assumed command of the *Juniata*, the vessel was a unit of the European Squadron. Once again Greene and Worden crossed paths, as Worden was flag officer of the squadron at that time. In November 1875, Worden was ordered to send the *Juniata* to Port Royal, South Carolina, where a large force of warships was being concentrated because of trouble with Spain over Cuba. When the crisis ended and the vessel returned to European waters early in the new year, Greene was detached to take command of the *Monongahela*. For nearly a year and a half, Greene commanded the *Monongahela*, which served as a training ship on the Atlantic coast. The vessel was used primarily to carry midshipmen on their annual cruises.

His final sea duty came in 1882, when he was appointed to command the *Despatch*, a converted steamer purchased and fitted out for dispatch duty because of her speed. By the time Greene took her over, however, she had been converted into a training ship to instruct cadet engineers for the Naval Academy. She was also occasionally used for ceremonial functions by the President, the Secretary of the Navy, other members of the cabinet, congressmen, etc. In 1884, Greene was detached from the *Despatch* and ordered to the Portmouth Navy Yard as executive officer. On December 11, 1884, while at the Navy Yard, Greene committed suicide.

The Concord Evening *Monitor* of Concord, New Hampshire, wrote in its December 12, 1884, issue,

> Commander S. Dana Greene, U.S. Navy, equipment officer in the Portsmouth navy yard, and one of the most popular officers in the service, committed suicide Thursday afternoon. His lifeless body was discovered in the Franklin shiphouse at this yard, with a bullet wound in the head, and a 38 caliber revolver in his right hand. He had been observed to act strangely for some time, and had been watched for fear that he might take his own life. As executive officer of the *Monitor* in the fight with the *Merrimack*, he took an important part in that encounter. Anxiety over the preparation of a literary work on that subject is thought to have resulted in temporary insanity.

A biographical sketch of Greene in the *Dictionary of American Biography* states that "the cause assigned for this act was anxiety over an article on the engagement between the *Monitor* and *Merrimac* that he was preparing for publication." Presumably this is the article that was published posthumously in *The Century Magazine* and later in *Battles and Leaders of the Civil War*. In March 1895, Captain (later Rear Admiral) Alfred T. Mahan, one of Greene's classmates, wrote, "My wife wrote me that a post mortem in Dana Greene's case showed an abcess [sic] at the base of the brain which could account for any degree of insanity." Years later Mahan wrote again about Greene's unfortunate death. "There was, I think, some specific physical course that induced the brain trouble, which was aggrevated [sic] by a controversy he got into over the *Monitor* and *Merimac* fight."

No specific information has been located to suggest what the "controversy" was. There is some evidence, however, to indicate that it concerned Greene's conduct while in command of the *Monitor*'s guns and after Worden's wound, while he commanded the *Monitor* himself. In March 1886, Worden wrote a newspaper reporter that he would not engage in "newspaper controversy over the fight" but added that Greene's conduct had been satisfactory.

On more than one occasion Worden defended his former executive officer. During the war, he became aware of criticism of Greene's conduct during the engagement and wrote to the Secretary of the Navy that "Lieutenant Greene...handled the guns with great courage, coolness, and skill; and throughout the engagement...he exhibited an earnest devotion to duty unsurpassed in my experience."

In retrospect, it seems probable that Greene allowed this criticism to weigh heavily over the years. He clearly expected to receive command of a vessel during the war, and it is possible that he blamed his failure to receive the coveted command on this criticism. The emotional strain occasioned by preparing the article apparently was a factor in his death, although the evidence suggests that he was in poor health at the time.

Greene's death personified his life. He was perhaps the most unfortunate of the *Monitor*'s commanding officers. Greene married twice. His first wife died in 1874 after eleven years of marriage. His son, Samuel Dana Greene II, entered the Naval Academy and graduated in 1883 at the head of the class. A most promising career was cut short in 1900 when he and his wife drowned while ice skating. They apparently fell unseen and unheard through the cracked ice.

What evidence we have suggests that Greene was a competent naval officer. He was respected by his peers and no criticism of his conduct by them has been found.

Figure 3. Thomas Oliver Selfridge, Jr. (Photograph courtesy of U.S. Naval Historical Center).

THOMAS OLIVER SELFRIDGE, JR.

During the evening of March 10, 1862, a young lieutenant, Thomas Oliver Selfridge, Jr., was ushered into the *Monitor*'s wardroom where he found the ship's officers "sitting together with Lieutenant Greene." Selfridge informed Greene that he had been "ordered to command the *Monitor*." Thus began Selfridge's brief tour (four days) in command of the most famous vessel in the United States Navy at that time.

Thomas O. Selfridge, Jr., was the son of a distinguished officer in the navy, Captain Thomas Oliver Selfridge, Sr. Selfridge, Sr., entered the navy in 1818 and commanded a number of ships and naval stations before retiring in 1866. He died in 1903 at the age of ninety-eight, one of the oldest officers ever carried on the Navy List. The British Admiralty ordered their ships and stations to fly their flags at half mast in memory of Selfridge, Sr., the oldest admiral in the world when he died.

Selfridge, Jr., was born on February 6, 1836, in Charlestown, Massachusetts. Selfridge would later write in his *Memoirs* that virtually from the cradle it was assumed that he would follow his father in a naval career. His formal training commenced when he entered the Naval Academy at Annapolis in 1851. Selfridge was the first officer to receive a diploma under the permanent Naval Academy system when he graduated in 1854 at the head of his class of six. Because of the need for more junior officers, his class graduated a year early.

Soon after graduation, Midshipman Selfridge reported on board the *Independence* in New York City, preparing for a cruise as flagship to the Pacific Squadron. During the following two years, the *Independence* sailed around the Horn to California, and from there to the Hawaiian Islands, Samoa, Chile, and Panama. Josiah Tattnall, who would later command the Confederate ironclad *Virginia*, was captain of the *Independence*. Selfridge referred to Tattnall as a gunnery "sharp" and gave him credit for developing his expertise in gunnery. Selfridge, throughout his career, would place a considerable emphasis on gunnery practice. The young midshipman apparently impressed his commanding officer, for he was assigned as a regular watch and division officer, the only midshipman other than "passed midshipmen" so assigned.

In the fall of 1856, he was ordered to Washington, D.C., where he successfully passed his examination for promotion to passed midshipman. Two years later, he would be advanced to the rank of master.

In January 1857, Selfridge was ordered to the Coast Survey schooner *Nautilus*. There were not enough billets available for the entire officer corp in the late 1850s. Therefore a large number of officers were assigned to coast survey work, engaged in charting the rivers and harbors throughout the United States. The *Nautilus*, with Selfridge as acting master, surveyed the Rappahannock River in Virginia and the Hudson in New York before he received orders as master to the sloop *Vicennes* in the African Squadron. Survey work was considered tedious and boring by most naval officers, but it did provide them with much-needed experience in handling small vessels.

The African Squadron had been established in the 1840s to aide in the suppression of the foreign slave trade. Because of the prevalence of yellow fever and malaria and the lack of attractive liberty ports, the African Squadron was universally disliked throughout the service. It was considered the least desirable of all the foreign stations. For two and a half years, Selfridge served on the *Vincennes*. He described that cruise as

> very unpleasant, on account not only of the climate and the isolation, but also the unsociability, not to say tyranny, of our captain. All of the ship's officers were constantly harassed by him and often placed under suspension. My principal duty was that of navigator, though it frequently was necessary to take a watch when the other officers were sick.

Selfridge concluded his account by saying that it "was the most unpleasant one of my experience."

In the summer of 1860 Selfridge was promoted to lieutenant and shortly afterwards was ordered to the frigate *Cumberland*, flagship of the Home Squadron. The Home Squadron included all commissioned vessels stationed on the Atlantic and Gulf coasts.

Selfridge was on the *Cumberland* when the Civil War began. In April, the frigate was at the Gosport Navy Yard at Norfolk for repairs. When the yard was abandoned, Selfridge was detailed with a small number of men from the *Cumberland* to destroy equipment and facilities, to keep them out of Confederate hands. As the yard was set on fire the *Cumberland*, in tow of a small steamer, was taken down the mouth of the Elizabeth River and out into Hampton Roads.

The *Cumberland* was employed in blockading the entrance to the James and Elizabeth rivers throughout the late spring and early summer of 1861. After a brief refit at the Boston Navy Yard, she was ordered to join the naval force off Hatteras Inlet, North Carolina. In August the *Cumberland*, along with other Union naval vessels, bombarded the two forts guarding the inlet. When the forts surrendered, the frigate returned to Hampton Roads and anchored in the mouth of the James River. There she was joined by the *Congress* to blockade the river. Six months later the two vessels were still on station near the river's mouth when the Confederate ironclad *Virginia* made her appearance.

At 12.45 P.M. on March 8, 1862, lookouts on both the *Cumberland* and *Congress* observed three Confederate vessels steaming out of the Elizabeth River. As they got nearer, it was discovered that one of the vessels was the *Virginia*, converted by the southerners from the wooden sloop-of-war *Merrimack*. Both ships promptly beat to quarters and cleared for action.

The Union vessels had ample time to prepare for battle, because the slow-moving ironclad took slightly more than an hour to steam within firing range. The *Virginia*'s commanding officer intended to ram the *Cumberland* first--she had a much heavier battery than the *Congress*--then turn on the *Congress*. The *Cumberland* was anchored 800 yards from the shore, lying athwart the river with her bow outward, an unfortunate position because she could not be swung to meet her opponent. The *Cumberland* opened fire as soon as her guns could be brought to bear; the *Virginia* replied and, as the ironclad closed, the two vessels continued to exchange fire. The *Cumberland* definitely received the worst of it. Shots bounced off the ironclad's armor while shells from the *Virginia* penetrated the Union vessel's fragile hull and exploded among her crew. After raking the helpless wooden vessel for a few minutes, the *Virginia* rammed the *Cumberland*'s starboard side, crushing her hull directly below the berth deck. Upon impact the ironclad fired one of her bow rifles into the stricken ship, killing ten men. The *Cumberland* began immediately to settle by the bow with a list to port. She nearly dragged the *Virginia* down, too, for the ram had stuck in the victim's hull. However, the ram broke and the ironclad was able to back clear.

During the engagement Selfridge was in charge of the frigate's forward battery of six guns. He wrote in his *Memoirs* that even after the *Virginia* had rammed the Union warship and she was obviously sinking, the *Cumberland*'s acting commanding officer, Lieutenant George N. Morris, refused to surrender. For nearly half an hour, until it was impossible to elevate the guns, he continued to fight. "There were very few men left in the first division which I commanded for so long," wrote Selfridge.

> Not a gun's crew could be mustered from the six crews of brave fellows who had gone into action so confident in their ship only three quarters of an hour before....The appearance of the gun deck forward at this time can never be forgotten. It was covered with the dead and wounded and slippery with blood. Some guns were left run in their last shot; rammers and sponges, broken and powder-blackened, lay in every direction; the large galley was demolished and its scattered contents added to the general blood-spattered confusion... .Meanwhile the water had been rapidly gaining in spite of the efforts of the after division which had been sent to the pumps....The writer started aft, and on the way the ship gave a lurch forward, and water commenced pouring in through the bridle ports....The order was passed for 'every man to look out for himself'; an order never given until the last extremity....I was one of the last to leave the main deck, the water then being up to the main hatch....The peril was imminent, and, throwing off coat and sword, I squeezed through a gun port. In doing so, however, the heel of my boot became jammed against the port sill by the gun, which, from a position partially inboard had slid outboard by the listing of the ship. For a few precious moments it seemed as though I must be carried down with the rapidly sinking ship; but with much difficulty, from a bent position I finally succeeded in wrenching off the boot-heel and thus freeing my foot. Then jumping into the icy water, encumbered by boots and clothing, I swam to the launch astern and was picked up exhausted.

After Selfridge and the other survivors had reached the beach, according to one account, he saw the *Cumberland*'s flag still flying at the masthead and with a small group of volunteers returned to the sinking ship and retrieved the flag. Another account by one of the *Cumberland*'s officers mentioned that, while the survivors were standing on the beach,

> the Merrimack again opened fire on the Congress. The shells were flying over our heads in a very uncomfortable manner, when we met Lieutenant Selfridge near some large trees. A shell came whizzing along, passing over our heads and the pilot and I involuntarily ducked our heads and each of us got behind a good-sized tree, seeing which Lieutenant Selfridge, who was very much affected, said, 'Don't dodge, I wish one would kill me; I'd rather be killed than be whipped....'

Selfridge did not mention either in his *Memoirs*. He did write,

> Furious over the loss of the ship in which I had taken such intense pride, shivering with cold from soaking wet and scanty clothing, the reaction from the long endured, frightful, experience of battle impelled me to tears, and I sobbed like a child.

That evening Selfridge remained on the beach and the following day he, along with thousands of others lining both sides of Hampton Roads, witnessed the *Monitor-Virginia* engagement. After the battle was over, the *Cumberland* and *Congress* survivors were taken out to the *Roanoke*, the flagship of Captain John Marston, the senior officer present. Leave was granted to the survivors, including Selfridge. Before he was able to depart, however,

> a message came from Mr. Fox, the Assistant Secretary of the Navy, who had come down from Washington on receipt of news of the *Merrimac* episode, that he wished to see me. Captain Marston had recommended me for the command of the *Monitor* in place of Lieutenant Worden, who had been wounded in the fight, and the Secretary offered me the honor. . . .I thanked him for his confidence and replied that, 'if the *Merrimac* comes out, the *Monitor* will be on hand.'

Selfridge, after reporting on board that evening accompanied by Engineer Alban L. Stimers, spent more than four hours thoroughly examining the *Monitor* from stem to stern. Selfridge would only command the *Monitor* for four days and says very little about this period in his *Memoirs* He did write that

> Early next morning [the day after assuming command] we proceeded to a position off the mouth of the Elizabeth River, and remained without being rewarded by a sight of the *Merrimack*.

He did mention in a letter written in 1891 that he was responsible for the sloping pilot house that replaced the box-like one in which Worden had been wounded during the battle with the *Virginia*. Paymaster Keeler wrote on March 13, 1862, "We are making some slight repairs ourselves, particularly in the pilot house, which proved, as I thought, to be the weakest and I might say the only vulnerable spot about us."

On March 13 Lieutenant William N. Jeffers was ordered to relieve Selfridge in command of the *Monitor*. Selfridge wrote that

> Mr. Fox again sent for me and stated that, previous to his having ordered me to command the *Monitor*, he had sent a dispatch boat to Commodore [Louis] Goldsborough, the Commander-in-Chief of the fleet, who was then off the coast of North Carolina, directing that Lieutenant Jeffers be sent at once to command the *Monitor*. Mr. Jeffers had just arrived and the Secretary was obviously embarrassed at the situation. This was relieved by my pointing out that Lieutenant Jeffers was many years the senior, and that under the circumstances I could have no objection to his superceding me.

Selfridge then went on a month's leave and upon returning to Hampton Roads was given command of the *Illinois*, a large coastal steamer chartered by the government. Again the command only lasted a few days, as the vessel's charter was revoked. He then became flag lieutenant on the staff of Flag Officer Louis N. Goldsborough, in command of the North Atlantic Blockading Squadron. In this position, Selfridge carried out a number of tasks including taking orders to various ship commanders and, after the occupation of Norfolk, the destruction of abandoned Confederate batteries in the vicinity of the port.

In July Goldsborough resigned as flag officer and Selfridge journeyed to Washington, D.C., to obtain orders, hopefully to command a ship. Once again it was the Assistant Secretary of the Navy, Fox, who responded to the young officer's plea. Fox offered him command of the most unorthodox vessel in the navy at that time, the *Alligator*. The *Alligator,* which "resembled a whale in external form," was a submarine. The vessel was built in Philadelphia during the fall and winter of 1861-62. She was 45 feet in length and 4 feet 6 inches in the beam, built along the lines of a steamship boiler with a riveted hull. Her propulsion consisted of eight oars on each side. On June 13, 1862, the navy accepted the submarine from her builder. Shortly afterwards, she was towed to Hampton Roads, but no suitable "target" could be found. Goldsborough considered the *Alligator* useless and obtained permission to send her to the Washington Navy Yard for further testing. The submarine was still at the yard when Selfridge received orders to command her.

Selfridge commanded the *Alligator* less than two weeks. He carried out a series of tests and on August 8 reported to the Department that "the enterprise is a failure." He had difficulty in controlling the vessel while submerged and stressed that she was extremely slow on the surface, unable to stem the tide. Selfridge and his entire crew, all volunteers, requested transfer and on August 9, he was ordered to take his men to Cairo, Illinois. (The *Alligator* was later lost off Hatteras while being towed to Charleston.) At Cairo, Selfridge received the good news that he had been promoted to lieutenant commander and also that he was ordered to command the *Cairo*.

Selfridge took command of the *Cairo* at Memphis, Tennessee. She was 175 feet long, 51 1/2 feet in the beam with a 6-foot draft. Her battery of thirteen guns was enclosed in an iron armored casemate. The *Cairo* was one of seven gunboats of the type called the City Class because they were named after western river ports.

During the first three months of Selfridge's command, the *Cairo* patrolled the Mississippi River, occasionally exchanging rifle and cannon fire with Confederate guerillas. On November 21, Rear Admiral David Porter, in command of the Mississippi Squadron, detailed the *Cairo* to an expedition being formed to attack Vicksburg, Mississippi. As a preliminary to this expedition, the *Cairo* was ordered to ascend the Yazoo River, which flowed into the Mississippi ten miles above Vicksburg, and clear the stream of mines. On December 12, 1862, Selfridge in the *Cairo* led a small flotilla of gunboats up the winding Yazoo. At approximately mid-morning the *Cairo* struck two mines. Her bow was lifted out of the water by the explosion. As the vessel began to settle, Selfridge shoved her into the bank. In twelve minutes the *Cairo* was completely submerged except for her stacks.

Although no lives were lost and only a few men were slightly wounded, the loss of the *Cairo* earned Selfridge considerable criticism. A fellow officer wrote, "On December 12 Lieutenant Commander Selfridge. . .found two torpedoes and removed them by placing his vessel over them." Admiral Porter informed the Navy Department of the vessel's loss and remarked that the *Cairo* "incautiously proceded too far ahead. . . when the torpedo exploded under her." He accused Selfridge of disobeying orders and added, "My own opinion is that due caution was not observed." The admiral, however, apparently impressed with Selfridge's aggressiveness, later withdrew his censure: "I can see in it nothing more than one of the accidents of war arising from a zealous disposition on the part of the commanding officer to perform his duty." When Selfridge reported to Porter on his flagship, he asked the admiral if a court of inquiry was to be held. Porter replied, "Court! I have no time to order courts. I can't blame an officer who puts his ship close to the enemy. Is there any other vessel you would like to have?" Selfridge was then ordered to assume command of the *Conestoga*, whose commanding officer had recently been detached because of ill health.

Porter informed the Navy Department, "I have put. . .[Selfridge] in command of the *Conestoga*. . .trusting that he may be more fortunate hereafter, this being the second time during the war that his vessel has gone down under him."

Selfridge commanded the side wheeler for five months. During most of this period she patroled the Mississippi River in the vicinity of the Arkansas and White rivers. Porter had divided up the Mississippi River and its tributaries into areas of responsibility and assigned units of his squadron to designated areas. The vessels were to patrol their assigned areas and protect shipping. According to Selfridge, his most notable achievement while in command of the *Conestoga* was to change the course of the Mississippi River. At the mouth of the Arkansas River was a long, narrow point projecting into the Mississippi, making an eighteen-mile turn necessary to get around it. This had become a favorite spot for guerillas to attack transports. One morning Selfridge noticed that much of the neck was flooded because of unusually high water and came to the conclusion that, by digging a small ditch linking the flooded water, the channel might be diverted. He put his crew to work with shovels and a small ditch was dug. It worked. By the following morning, the Mississippi was rapidly cutting through the neck and within a few weeks it was wide and deep enough for vessels to follow that channel.

On the whole, however, Selfridge found his duty "monotinous, and. . .rather irksome, particularly since I felt that the unfortunate loss of the *Cairo* had kept me from participating in [the expedition against Vicksburg]." In May 1863, the *Conestoga* needed to go north for repairs. Selfridge and his crew were transferred to the side-wheel gunboat *Manitou*. Less that two weeks after taking over the *Manitou*, he heard that General William T. Sherman had requested a battery of naval guns. The guns were to be landed and installed in positions to be used against the Confederates defending Vicksburg. Selfridge, anxious for more active service, immediately volunteered to command the guns. Porter approved and the *Manitou*'s two 8-inch guns were landed early in June. From then until the end of the siege and surrender of Vicksburg, the battery fired constantly on Confederate positions. More than a thousand rounds were fired and at least two Confederate cannon were put out of action. On the first of July, four days before the town's surrender, Selfridge was ordered to return to the *Conestoga*, which had rejoined the naval force near Vicksburg.

Shortly after resuming command of the *Conestoga*, Porter ordered Selfridge to lead a raid up the Red River. In addition to the *Conestoga* his force consisted of the gunboats *Manitou*, *Rattler*, *Forest Rose*, *Petrel*, and *Curlew*. For the first time, Selfridge was appointed to command an expedition. The object was to capture cotton and supplies as well as to disperse any Confederate forces along the river. The expedition was most successful. Entering the Red River, the gunboats turned into the Black River and afterwards into the Tensas River. Selfridge's small flotilla also reached Lake Tensas and the Little Red River, another tributary of the Red. Four steamers were destroyed, together with a large quantity of ammunition and provisions.

After this expedition, the *Conestoga* returned to patrolling the Mississippi River. On March 8, 1864, she collided with the USS *General Price* and sank in about four minutes. " Thus for the third time in the war, I had had my ship suddenly sunk under me," Selfridge wrote in his *Memoirs* . He added, "It is a strange coincident [sic] that the name of these ships all begin with the letter 'C'." Admiral Porter, in some disgust, said, "Well, Selfridge, you do not seem to have much luck with the top of the alphabet." Selfridge was then placed in command of the ironclad *Osage*, far from the "top of the alphabet."

He assumed command of the *Osage* two days after losing the *Conestoga*. The *Osage* was a river monitor, but unlike other monitors, she and her two sister ships were propelled by stern wheels. Unfortunately their wheels, protected by armored casings, made it impossible for the turrets to turn a full 360 degrees. The *Osage* was an unusual-looking vessel with virtually nothing showing above the waterline but the turret, the iron-plated house for the stern paddle wheel, and the tall thin stacks.

Shortly after Selfridge took her over, the *Osage* joined other warships in Admiral Porter's squadron on the Red River expedition. On January 4, 1864, Major General Henry W. Hallack wrote Major General Nathaniel P. Banks, "General Sherman and Steel agree with me in opinion that the Red River is the shortest and best...base of operations against Texas." Banks was ordered to "operate in that direction," as soon as there was "sufficient water." Late in March, Bank's army of approximately 36,000 men started towards Shreveport, their line of march paralleling the Red River and Porter's squadron of thirteen gunboats. Passage up the narrow and crooked river was difficult and dangerous; the water was low and at places obstructed. Near Alexandria, approximately halfway to Shreveport, there were rapids, choked with rocks which seriously impeded navigation. Taking advantage of a rise in the river, Porter's vessels, including the *Osage*, passed through the rapids but could go little farther. On April 8-9, 1864, Banks' army was defeated and turned back in two battles. His troops began to retire back downstream and Porter had no choice but to do the same with his vessels. The admiral left Selfridge in charge of a rear guard division of four light ironclads several miles above Alexandria, while the rest of the squadron passed through the rapids above Alexandria. Because the river was so low a dam had be be built to enable the gunboats to pass throught the rapids. Selfridge's vessels were to prevent any Confederate effort to attack the squadron while this was going on. All but one of Porter's large gunboats made it through the rapids safely, followed shortly afterwards by the four light ironclads.

With the end of the unfortunate Red River expedition, the *Osage* returned to patrolling the Mississippi. However, in May Selfridge was given command of a new vessel, the recently completed ram *Vindicator*. He also remained in command of a division of gunboats which had the responsibility for patrolling a small segment of the river. By the summer of 1864, nearly all Confederate resistance, including guerilla attacks, had ceased. Selfridge, bored with the lack of activity, requested a transfer. Admiral Porter had recently been ordered to command the North Atlantic Blockading Squadron and intervened to get Selfridge sent to this squadron.

In October Selfridge was ordered to command the gunboat *Huron*, a small vessel of 700 tons with a battery of one 11-inch gun and a 30-pounder Parrott. Shortly after he assumed the command, the *Huron* was ordered to join the blockade off the Cape Fear River in North Carolina. The Cape Fear connected the port of Wilmington with the Atlantic Ocean. By 1864 Wilmington had become the most important center of blockade running in the southern states. Two forts, Caswell and Fisher, guarded the river mouth. Fort Fisher was considered by many to be the most powerful fort in the Confederacy. The navy had more than once urged that the forts be seized by amphibious assault, but until the fall of 1864 the army was unable or unwilling to provide troops. In the fall, however, priority was given to attacking Fort Fisher. The army made troops available and Admiral Porter assembled a powerful fleet to provide support.

On Christmas Eve, 1864, Porter's fleet bombarded the fort, firing more than 20,000 shells. The *Huron* participated in the attack. The bombardment, however, proved fruitless. The army commander, Major General Benjamin Butler, refused to land his troops. Porter, chagrined at this failure, immediately made plans to launch a second attack. On January 12, 1865, his fleet once again opened fire on the fort. During the following days more than 8,000 troops under Major General Alfred H. Terry landed under the fire of Porter's guns. On Sunday, January 15, 2,000 sailors and marines landed and attacked the seaward face of the fort while Terry's men assaulted from the land. Selfridge, in the thick of things as usual, commanded one of the units of bluejackets and marines in the landing party. He later wrote,

> At a preconcerted signal the sailors sprang forward to the assault closely following the water's edge. . . . We were opened upon in front by. . .artillery. . .and by the fire of a thousand rifles. Though many dropped rapidly under this fire, the column never faltered [until]. . .the head halted to allow the rear to come up. The halt was fatal. As the writer aproached with [his] division he shouted to his men to come on. . .but looking back he discovered that his whole command, with few exceptions, had stopped. . .the situation was a very grave one. The rush of sailors was over; they were packed like sheep in a pen, while the enemy was crowding the ramparts not forty yards away. . . .Flesh and blood could not long endure being killed in this slaughter, and the rear of the sailors broke, followed by the whole body.

Although Porter blamed the marines for this repulse, claiming that they should have provided covering fire, Selfridge disagreed. "The mistake was," he wrote, "in expecting a body of sailors, collected hastily from different ships. . .armed with swords and pistols, to stand against veteran soldiers armed with rifles and bayonets."

Despite the failure of the sailors, Fort Fisher fell to Terry's troops. A few days later Caswell also fell, opening the river to Porter's ships. Selfridge, who had returned to the *Huron* after the survivors of the landing party had been re-embarked, was ordered to anchor his ship in the mouth of the Cape Fear River. The *Huron* was fortunate enough to capture two blockade runners that had entered the river, not suspecting that the forts had fallen. After Wilmington was occupied by Federal troops, the *Huron* was ordered to the James River to cooperate with Union forces moving on Richmond. The gunboat participated in no action, however, and she was still in the river when Richmond surrendered early in April 1865. The news of Jefferson Davis' flight led Porter to order Selfridge with the *Huron* to Key West, Florida, to intercept the Confederate president if he tried to flee the country in that direction. After this, the *Huron* returned to New York City and was placed out of commission.

Selfridge had spent virtually the entire Civil War period on active service, most of it in combat zones. He had participated in numerous engagements, had had three ships sunk under him, and had been mentioned frequently in reports to the Department. As a naval officer who served with him wrote, Selfridge "has lived a good while for a young man." He was twenty-nine years old when the war ended.

Upon being detached from the *Huron*, Selfridge was ordered to report as executive officer to the *Hartford*, at that time preparing to leave for the Asiatic station. He requested shore duty in order to get married and was assigned to the Naval Academy as an instructor in the Department of Seamanship. In the fall of 1865 he married Ellen F. Shepley. They would have four sons. She died in 1905 and two years later he married Gertrude Wildes. While at the academy Selfridge was placed in command of the old *Macedonian*, which had been relegated to a training ship for midshipmen during the summer months. Practice cruises were made along the Atlantic coast and to Europe. A junior officer on the *Macedonian* wrote that Selfridge "was an excellent officer, and while under his command the old *Macedonian* was a model in making passage from port to port."

After three years of what Selfridge described as "very pleasant duty" at the Naval Academy, he was ordered to command the steam gunboat *Nipsic*. Selfridge's tour on the *Nipsic* lasted nearly two years, most of which was spent in the West Indies. At that time the United States was considering the establishment of a naval base in the Caribbean and Selfridge investigated possible sites in Cuba, Santa Domingo, and Haiti.

In December 1869, he was promoted to commander and ordered to conduct a survey of the Isthmus of Darien for an interoceanic canal. Selfridge would lead three expeditions to the Darien region between 1870 and 1873. Enduring unfriendly inhabitants, tropical fevers, rampaging rivers, and at times inpenetrable vegetation, Selfridge's small command explored all the country south of Panama to the headwaters of the Airato River in South America. The expeditions also surveyed a route that was considered feasible for a canal to link the Atlantic with the Pacific. For several years Selfridge would push for the adoption of his proposed route but with no success. For his work on the Darien Survey, Selfridge was awarded the decoration of the Legion of Honor of France and made an honorary member of the Royal Geographical Society of Belgium. He was also invited by Ferdinand de Lesseps to attend a congress on interoceanic canals in Paris.

After a three-year tour at the Boston Navy Yard, Selfridge was given command of the *Enterprise* in 1878 and ordered to survey the Amazon and Madeira rivers. The object was to prove the navigability of the great South American river system and open the interior of Brazil to American commerce. After completing this mission, the *Enterprise* was ordered to join the European Squadron for a two-year tour.

In November 1880, he was promoted to captain and ordered to take charge of the Naval Torpedo Station at Newport, Rhode Island. In the late 1860s Robert Whitehead, an Englishman, had developed an automotive torpedo. Whitehead torpedoes were used extensively during the Russo-Turkish War of 1877-1878 by the Russian navy, which used small fast "torpedo boats" to lauch attacks against large vessels. The Russian success persuaded the U.S. Navy to experiment with Whitehead torpedoes, and the station at Newport was established for this purpose. During the four years that Selfridge commanded the station, numerous experiments with torpedoes, torpedo nets, and torpedo-carrying craft were conducted. Selfridge considered that his experiments led to the navy's adopting these weapons.

In 1885 he was given command of the screw-sloop *Omaha*, which left in the spring of that year for an extended tour of duty with the Asiatic Squadron. An incident occurred during this cruise that resulted in Selfridge being court martialed. While in Japanese waters he held target practice, and a Japanese man was injured when he picked up an unexploded shell fired at a cliff by the *Omaha*. An unusual sequence of events followed. Selfridge's report on the incident resulted in his detachment from command of the *Omaha* and being ordered to Washington, D.C. The Secretary of the Navy ordered him back to Japan, where an inquiry would be held; and finally Selfridge himself demanded a court martial. He was acquitted by the court.

In 1889 Selfridge was ordered to Washington as a member of the Board of Inspection and Survey. The board at that time was involved in conducting trials on some of the first steel ships in the navy. He was then ordered to head a commission to select a site for a navy yard in Puget Sound on the west coast. Brementon was recommended and approved. In 1890 Selfridge was appointed commandant of the Boston Navy Yard and was still in command of the yard in 1894, when he was promoted to commodore.

In 1895 Selfridge was ordered to command the European Squadron. He received this prestigeous command because no rear admirals were available and he was in line for promotion to that rank. He was commissioned a rear admiral the following year.

The European Squadron was the successor to the Mediterranean Squadron and had been established during the Civil War. It was the most popular of the distant squadrons because of the attractive liberty ports. Selfridge himself would refer to his tour with the squadron as "almost like yachting."

When Selfridge assumed command, the squadron consisted of two armored cruisers, the *Marblehead* and the *San Francisco*. Shortly after taking over the squadron in November, he was ordered to the Ottoman Empire "to personally investigate and report fully on the danger to American missionaries." The danger referred to concerned Turkish atrocities against Armenians. American missionaries had established schools, hospitals, and churches in a number of Armenian villages and had reported to diplomatic and church officials that they were in some danger. The Armenian massacres in Anatolia and other parts of the Ottoman Empire had caused a storm of protest in Europe and the United States. It was fear for the lives of the missionaries in Turkey that prompted the United States government to order warships to the eastern Mediterranean. Even before Selfridge arrived to command the squadron, the *Marblehead* was patrolling off the Ottoman coast.

Shortly after he arrived in the Near East, Selfridge reported that the missionaries were, in his opinion, in no immediate danger. Nevertheless, apparently under pressure from missionary interests in the United States, a third armored cruiser, the *Minneapolis*, was ordered to join the European Squadron in the eastern Mediterranean. Early in June 1895, Selfridge received instructions to concentrate his squadron at Alexandria, Syria, to evacuate all Americans and to "land a force," if necessary. The Americans, mostly missionaries, refused to take refuge on the warships and Selfridge continued to insist that they were in no immediate danger.

In the spring of 1896, Selfridge departed with two of his vessels, planning to attend the coronation of Czar Nicholas II. The *Marblehead* was left in the eastern Mediterranean to evacuate Americans if necessary. In May the squadron sailed for Kronstadt. There the admiral and many of his officers journeyed to Moscow, where they participated in the pomp and pageantry surrounding the coronation of the last Romanov ruler of Imperial Russia. The squadron remained a month in Russian waters and then visited Denmark and England before returning to the eastern Mediterranean in August. Selfridge never changed his opinion concerning the lack of danger for the missionaries. He was also critical of the policy of deploying the European Squadron in Turkish waters for extended periods. Nevertheless, he was instructed to keep at least one of his vessels in the eastern Mediteranean at all times.

Admiral Selfridge's tour in command of the European Squadron was scheduled to end in August 1897, but the department agreed to allow him to remain until he reached the age of statutory retirement, which was sixty-two. On February 6, 1898, only a couple of months before war broke out with Spain, Selfridge hauled down his flag from the *San Francisco* and relinquished command of the squadron. This ended a career of forty-seven years in the navy.

Selfridge was considered an excellent squadron commander by his officers, but his "by the book" or no-nonsense attitude was at times considered to be excessive by subordinates. As a squadron commander, he personally examined the ships' logs, and when a discrepancy was found, the commanding officer would be reprimanded. Even spelling was corrected. He frequently wrote his commanders, expressing disapproval of any actions that deviated even slightly from regulations. He personally conducted weekly inspections of the vessels under his command, writing long, detailed reports of their conditions. Should one man fail inspection, he would cancel liberty for the entire ship's crew. On one occasion he went into a detailed explanation of how to clean and paint the *San Francisco* because "I do not approve of the manner painting is done and paint work is treated." He constantly harassed his commanders about coal consumption. Although the regulation requiring that the amount of coal used be recorded in the ship's log had been abolished years before, Selfridge demanded daily coal reports, including explanations for the quantity expended.

After retiring, Selfridge lived in Washington, D.C. He died there on February 4, 1924, at the age of eighty-eight. Selfridge was an intelligent and gifted officer who rose to the height of his profession. His contemporaries quite early recognized his unusually intense ambition, or what Admiral Porter called his "search for fame." He more than likely was aided in his professional ambitions by important connections, particularly the fact that he was the son of a ranking officer in the navy. Nevertheless, it was not this but his courage, leadership, and seamanship that earned him respect from his peers and superiors. As Captain Dudley W. Know wrote in the introduction to Selfridge's *Memoirs*, published in 1924 shortly before the admiral died, Selfridge was an officer "who embod[ied] all the finest traditions of our Navy."

Figure 4. William Nicholson Jeffers. (Photograph courtesy of U.S. Naval Historical Center).

WILLIAM NICHOLSON JEFFERS

On March 12, 1862, a short, somewhat rotund officer boarded the *Monitor* while she was at anchor in Hampton Roads and informed Lieutenant Selfridge that he had been ordered to take command of the ironclad. That night the new commanding officer, Lieutenant William Nicholson Jeffers, thirty-eight years old, met his officers in the ship's wardroom. They were impressed with their new captain. Young Greene, who had the command briefly, told his parents that "Mr. Jeffers is everything desirable, talented, educated, and energetic and experienced in battle." Paymaster Keeler wrote his wife,

> Lieut. Jefers [sic] has been in most of the fights along the coast and it is very interesting as we sit at the table to hear him give his experience in the different fights--some of them he sets out in a very amusing light.

Keeler was not quite so "amused" with his new captain a few days later: "Things don't go as smoothly and pleasantly on board as when we had Capt. Worden. Our new Capt. is a rigid disciplinarian, of quick imperious temper and domineering disposition..." and added, "so far I have got along smoothly enough with Capt. Jeffers, but I am expecting every day that I may forget to touch my hat, or give him the deck in passing, or greviously offend him in some little point of etiquitte [sic], when I shall get a blast." The paymaster's regard for Jeffers would become increasingly critical even after he left the ironclad to assume another command. In July 1863, Keeler referred to Jeffers as "a brute of a Captain." The *Monitor*'s crew apparently was equally displeased with Jeffers. In April 1862, they addressed a letter to Worden urging his return as quickly as possible. Yet Jeffers was respected in the navy, and there is no evidence that he had abused his rank during his career to that date.

William Nicholson Jeffers was born on October 16, 1824, in Swedesboro, New Jersey, the son of John Ellis Jeffers, a lawyer, and Ruth Wescott Jeffers. His father's family were New Englanders, many of them seafarers, and this probably played a role in his decision to seek a naval career. He entered the navy as an acting midshipman on September 25, 1840. After serving on various vessels on the Atlantic coast, he was in 1841 assigned to the frigate *United States*, under orders to the Pacific as flagship for Commodore Thomas ap Catesby Jones. The *United States*, launched in 1797, was one of the oldest ships in the navy. Jeffers was referred to by another midshipman as one of twenty-eight "young gentlemen" who made the cruise to the Pacific. Jeffers sailed around the Horn on the old frigate and remained in the Pacific Squadron for five years.

Midshipman Jeffers participated in the seizure of Monterey, in upper California, when Commodore Jones erroneously believed that the United States was at war with Mexico. In 1843, the frigate visited Honolulu, Hawaii, where Herman Melville enlisted on board as an ordinary seaman. The *United States* was the *Neversink* of Melville's *White Jacket*. There is no hint in *White Jacket* that Jeffers is one of the midshipmen he describes as living in the steerage. In 1844 Jeffers was ordered to the newly created naval academy, where in 1846 he graduated fourth in a class of forty-seven.

That same year, 1846, Jeffers, still a midshipman, published a book, *The Armament of Our Ships of War*. This is the first evidence of Jeffers' interest in gunnery and naval ordnance, a fascination that would continue throughout his career, culminating with his appointment as chief of the Bureau of Ordnance.

Jeffers was ordered to the light draft steamer *Vixen* upon the outbreak of the Mexican War and would participate in the attack on the forts of Alvarado, in two attacks and the capture of Tobasco, in the capture of Tuspan, Coatzacoalco, and Laguna de Terminos, and in the siege and capture of Vera Cruz and the castle of San Juan d'Ulloa. Upon the recommendation of Josiah Sands, the *Vixen*'s commanding officer, Jeffers was promoted to passed midshipman in November 1847. Within three months, on February 2, 1848, the war came to an end with the signing of a peace treaty. The *Vixen* had been the flagship of Commodore Matthew C. Perry, who was impressed enough with Jeffers to later select him for the Japan expedition. Unfortunately the *Princeton*, to which he was assigned, was removed from the squadron after being declared "unfit."

After the Mexican War, Jeffers was stationed at the Naval Academy as instructor of mathematics. While there he wrote his second and third books, *Nautical Routine and Stowage, with Short Rules in Navigation* (in collaboration with J. M. Murphy), and *A Concise Treatise on the Theory and Practice of Naval Gunnery*. Jeffers had hoped to be assigned to train midshipmen in gunnery, but the Secretary of the Navy turned down his request. In fact, because there was no billet available, he was placed on "awaiting orders."

As with so many other junior officers in the navy, Jeffers turned to the Coast Survey for employment at sea. He remained with the survey on sea duty until he was ordered to the *Princeton* in 1852. On September 17, 1850, while on leave he married Lucie LeGrand Smith, the daughter of an army surgeon whom he had met while at Annapolis. They would have a son, who died at age seven, and a daughter.

The failure of the *Princeton* to be included in Perry's expedition persuaded Jeffers to obtain permission to join a party organized to survey Honduras for an "interoceanic railway." Jeffers apparently received a leave of absence from the navy and was employed by E. G. Squier, a former char´ge d'affaires of the United States in the republics of Central America. It was Squier who conceived the idea of such a railway and hired Jeffers to make the survey. In the introductions to *Notes on Central America . . .and the Proposed Inter-Oceanic Railway,* published by 1855 by Squier, Jeffers was recognized as a member of the expedition "with acknowledged scientific and practical ability." The expedition left the United States in February 1853, and by the end of the year Jeffers had surveyed from the Bay of Fonseca across to the Pacific. In 1857 he would take leave again and conduct a second survey in the area. Despite the survey's "positive results" and a lobbying campaign carried out for several years, the railway was never built, at least partly because of intense British-American rivalry in the area.

In 1854 Jeffers returned to naval service and was ordered to the Brazil Squadron. Jeffers served as acting master on first the *Alleghany* and the *Germantown* before being promoted to lieutenant and transferred to the *Water Witch*. In January 1855, when he reported on board as executive officer, the *Water Witch* was engaged in surveying the La Plata and Parana´ Rivers in South America. The *Water Witch*, Lieutenant Thomas Jefferson Page in command, was a small side-wheel steamer carrying a battery of only three small bronze howitzers. Within a few days after reporting on board, Page ordered Jeffers to take the steamer into the Alto Parana´ as far as the island of Apip´e to chart some rapids. This decision plunged Jeffers into an incident that created an international crisis and came close to involving the United States in a conflict.

In the middle of the nineteenth century the navy sponsored a number of expeditions to explore and survey bodies of water throughout the world. One of these was to the Rio de la Plata and its tributaries.. Page received command of the expedition and reached the La Plata on the *Water Witch* in 1853. The survey was carried out without incident until the fall of 1854, when difficulties developed between Paraguay's President Carlos Antonia Lopez and Page. In October, Lopez issued a decree forbidding "foreign vessels of war" from navigating the rivers of the Republic. Four months later, in violation of the decree, Page ordered Jeffers to proceed up the Parana´ River, which would carry him into Paraguayan territory.

On February 1, as the *Water Witch* attempted to pass the Paraguayan fort of Itapiru´, the vessel was fired upon after receiving several warnings in Spanish. The *Water Witch* was hit several times, the helmsman was killed and the tiller carried away before the vessel could steam out of range. Jeffers had returned the fire with his three small howitzers, but had done little damage. The American vessel returned back down river where Lieutenant Page was informed of the incident. Page attempted without success to persuade the flag officer of the Brazil Squadron to take punitive action. The *Water Witch*, again with Jeffers as executive officer, completed the survey, although the rivers above Ascuncion were closed to the Americans. In February 1856, the ship returned to the United States.

As one historian recently wrote, the *Water Witch* incident "seriously damaged diplomatic relations between the two countries. There were two American naval officers who helped create the *Water Witch* incident with their unorthodox behaviour." The two, of course, were Page and Jeffers, who according to this writer, displayed "ineptitude." "Jeffers," he wrote, "seemed to be even less tactful than his superior since he chose to ignore the warnings of the Commander of Fort Itapiru´." Another author agreed: "A large degree of the blame seems to lie upon the shoulders of Lt. Jeffers. . ." He added, "Jeffers seems to have been unduly pugnacious. . . ."

Ironically, neither officer was reprimanded by the Navy Department for his actions. In fact, Jeffers would later be commended while in command of the *Water Witch* for rescuing the Spanish warship *Carthagena* from being wrecked. In 1858, Congress passed a resolution permitting Jeffers to accept a sword of honor from the Queen of Spain for the rescue.

Jeffers' interest in gunnery had never wavered. The two books that he wrote on the subject, although not well known in the navy, were known and appreciated in the Bureau of Ordnance and Hydrography. In 1858 he was ordered to the sloop-of-war *Plymouth*. In 1856 this vessel had been assigned to Lieutenant Commander John A. Dahlgren as an experimental ordnance ship. The executive officer was Catesby ap R. Jones, later executive officer and commanding officer of the Confederate armorclad *Virginia* . As a young officer on the vessel, Jeffers had the opportunity to serve under the designer of the Dahlgren smoothbore gun, which would become the most popular naval gun used during the Civil War. Jeffers impressed Dahlgren with his intelligence and grasp of ballistics and other technical aspects of gunnery. He would be considered one of Dahlgren's proteges and an "expert" in ordnance after this.

Jeffers' next assignment was not so fortunate. In August 1859, he was ordered to the new steam sloop *Brooklyn,* with Captain David G. Farragut in command. Shortly after joining the ship, Jeffers became embroiled in a bitter quarrel with Farragut. The captain had apparently gone ashore with an overcoat over his uniform and Jeffers, upon passing him, failed to salute. Upon returning to the ship, Jeffers was informed "not to leave the ship except by special permission of the Captain." After a meeting, both Farragut and Jeffers wrote the Secretary of the Navy. Farragut preferred charges against Jeffers: "treating with contempt his superior officer; failure to salute him or recognize him as his commanding officer two or three times;" and "scandalous conduct tending to the destruction of good morals." Jeffers asked to be detached from the *Brooklyn* after explaining his account of the difficulty. Later Jeffers wrote what amounted to an apology to Farragut and by mutual agreement the Secretary of the Navy was requested to withdraw all the correspondence concerning the quarrel. What effect, if any, this had on Jeffers' career is not known. Early in 1860 the *Brooklyn* was sent to Mexico to carry the United States minister to that country. Shortly after arriving at Vera Cruz, the minister was ordered back to Washington. Before leaving, Farragut sent ashore a small force of twenty-two sailors and marines under Jeffers to protect the American consulate there. The

Brooklyn was detained until March, and when she arrived back in Vera Cruz, Jeffers was found to be ill with rheumatism. Jeffers, however, was apparently not ill enough to be detached from the ship. The *Brooklyn* was sent to Panama to land a party to explore a route across the Isthmus of Chiriqui. Jeffers was appointed hydrographer for the expedition. In the fall of 1860, Jeffers again became ill and was detached from the *Brooklyn*. He was still at home on sick leave when the Civil War broke out.

Immediately after the firing on Fort Sumter, Jeffers requested active service. He was ordered to take charge of the ordnance facility at the Norfolk Navy Yard, but the yard was evacuated and partially destroyed by Union forces before he could get there. He was then placed in command of the *Philadelphia*, a small side-wheel, iron-hulled steamer which had been operating as a trading vessel between Acquia Creek, Virginia, and Washington, D.C. On April 30, Jeffers took over the vessel with orders to carry troops and supplies to Fort Washington on the Potomac River. On May 11 he was instructed to load cargo and proceed to Philadelphia and New York City. The *Philadelphia* returned to Washington, D.C., two weeks later, after a rough voyage. Jeffers reported that "this steamer is in no respect suitable for outside service." Whether because of this report or damage to the *Philadelphia* sustained during the voyage, or simply because a trained naval officer was needed elsewhere, Jeffers was detached from the steamer immediately after reaching the Washington Navy Yard and assigned to the frigate *Roanoke*. The *Philadelphia*, despite Jeffers critical report, would go "outside" and remain on blockade duty for most of the war.

Jeffers would remain on the *Roanoke* for six months, participating in blockade duties from Hampton Roads, Virginia, to Charleston, South Carolina. In November 1861, he was ordered to command the side-wheel steamer *Underwriter*, which carried a battery of four guns.

Shortly after taking command, Jeffers was ordered with the *Underwriter*, accompanied by two tow-boats carrying stone-filled hulks, to scuttle the hulks in Ocracoke Inlet, blockading that entrance to the North Carolina sounds. In early February the *Underwriter* participated in the Battle of Roanoke Island. Flag Officer Louis N. Goldsborough was in command of the naval force of seventeen vessels, including Jeffers' gunboat, that provided fire support for Union troops as they landed on the island. The Confederates had not only fortified the island but six small gunboats contributed to the defense. The *Underwriter* engaged the Confederate vessels, but as they were above some obstructions in the channel and retired before the battle was over, little damage was done to them. On February 9, Goldsborough sent fourteen of his vessels, under the command of Commander S. C. Rowan, to occupy Elizabeth City, North Carolina, and cut communications through the Dismal Swamp and Chesapeake and Albemarle canals. This force, including the *Underwriter*, entered the Pasquotank River and engaged Confederate gunboats under Commodore William F. Lynch a few miles below Elizabeth City. The Confederate vessels were destroyed or captured with no losses to Rowan's command. Elizabeth City then surrendered.

The *Underwriter* then made a brief reconnaissance to Edenton before Jeffers was sent with a small force towing captured vessels to obstruct the Albemarle and Chesapeake Canal. Upon reaching the southern end, he discovered that the Confederates had already partially blocked it. He reported,

> On opening the reach of the [North] River leading to the canal, I discovered two small steamers and three schooners about a mile and a quarter up the canal, and that the mouth of the canal was obstructed. . . .I immediately moved up within a couple of hundred yards to the mouth of the canal, until all of the vessels grounded, and ordered the *Whitehead* to open fire with her nine-inch guns. . . .The steamers

> and schooners had left before we landed. . . .I
> completed the rebel work by sinking two schooners
> in the mouth of the canal.

Jeffers was praised by Rowan for his "usual zeal and intelligence" in closing the canal. He continued to command the *Underwriter* in North Carolina waters until the wounding of Worden in the *Monitor*'s engagement with the *Virginia*. He was then ordered by Flag Officer Goldsborough to take command of the *Monitor*.

Jeffers replaced Selfridge, who had been in command only four days. As mentioned earlier, Assistant Secretarty of the Navy Fox had appointed Selfridge to the command, unaware that Goldsborough, upon being informed of Worden's wounding, had instructed Jeffers to take the ironclad. As the appointment of a replacement commanding officer was the prerogative of the squadron commander, Fox had to inform Selfridge that Jeffers was to be the *Monitor*'s captain. Jeffers was selected by Goldsborough because he wanted an experienced officer in command of the *Monitor*, and because Jeffers was considered an ordnance expert and the flag officer felt that the turreted vessel needed an officer with intelligence and knowledge in gunnery.

Jeffers looked upon his new command as a challenge and a professional opportunity, particularly in gunnery. Paymaster Keeler told his wife that Jeffers and Chief Engineer Alban Stimers would frequently sit around the wardroom table discussing "ordnance, all kinds of projectiles, the build and shape of ships and strength of materials." "Chief Engineer Stimers and Capt. Jeffers are both men of scientific attainment," he added, "well educated and intelligent." In another letter, Keeler mentioned that "as an ordnance officer [Jeffers] is second to no one in the Service but Dahlgren." After commanding the ironclad slightly more than a month, including participating in one major engagement, Jeffers forwarded a thoughtful analysis of the defects in the monitor type and recommendations for improvements:

> I have hitherto refrained from making any official
> report relative to this vessel, as most of her
> prominent defects have been pointed out or
> discovered by Chief Engineer Stimers.

He then discussed in detail what he considered to be the more serious flaws in the *Monitor*. Not surprisingly the majority of the points that he stressed concerned gunnery. He emphasized that the captain could not control the guns from the pilot house; that the gunnery officer had to find his target through the "small aperture" or narrow sighting slit by rotating the turret back and forth; that he had more success in locating and hitting his target by exposing himself on the turret top, "roughly sight[ing]. . .by the lines of parallel plates" of the deck; that because of muzzle blast the guns could not be fired closer than thirty degrees of either side of the pilot house and because of possible rupture of the boilers, they could not be fired closer than fifty degrees of the stern. This significantly reduced the 360-degree theoretical field of fire to 200 degrees. He also pointed out that only one gun could be run out at a time and "the ports have not sufficient elevation to allow the guns to be pointed at a battery on an eminence." The vessel was inadequately ventilated; on one occasion heat in the turret reached 140 degrees during action. It was so intolerable that he had to send men out of the turret in order to recuperate. In conclusion Jeffers wrote,

> Notwithstanding the recent battle in Hampton Roads
> and the exploits of the plated gunboats in the Western
> rivers, I am of the opinion that protecting the guns
> and gunners does not, except in special cases,
> compensate for the greatly diminished quantity of
> artillery, slow speed, and inferior accuracy of fire;

> and that for general purposes wooden ships, shell guns, and forts, whether for offense of defense, have not yet been superseded.

Goldsborough forwarded this "highly important" report on to the Navy Department.

Jeffers was extremely perceptive about the monitor-type vessel, but apparently his strong reservations (agreed with by the majority of the officers who commanded monitor types during the war) were ignored. More than thirty monitors were built and in general their performance was unsatisfactory. He, of course, was wrong about iron-armored vessels vs. wooden vessels, but he was addressing the problems of the monitor type, having no experience in other types of armored vessels.

Jeffers would command the *Monitor* for more than four months (March 15 to August 18). For nearly half of that time, the Confederate ironclad *Virginia* was his major responsibility. On March 10, three days before Jeffers took command of the *Monitor*, Secretary of the Navy Welles sent a telegram to Flag Officer Goldsborough ordering "that the Monitor be not too much exposed and that in no event shall any attempt be made to proceed with her unattended to Norfolk." The secretary was convinced that the *Monitor* was the only thing that could prevent the *Virginia* from sallying forth and attacking the nation's capital or places along the eastern seaboard.

Although the threat was not real, the Confederate ironclad's presence weighed heavily on the mind of Major General George B. McClellan, commander of the Union army on the Virginia peninsula. Because of her presence, the James River was effectively closed to Union warships and transports, and the campaign to take Richmond was delayed. On March 12, McClellan telegraphed naval officials to inquire whether the *Monitor* could be relied upon to keep the *Virginia* in check. The general decided to shift his water communications to the York River and expected the navy to "watch and neutralize the Merrimac" and prevent the Confederates from threatening his operations. But by early April, McClellan's plans had been discovered and a small Confederate naval squadron made preparations to attack the Union gunboats and transports assembled in the York River. Before this attack could be mounted, the *Monitor* would have to be destroyed.

On March 30, Paymaster Keeler wrote his wife, "We still vainly watch the mouth of Elizabeth River, no Merrimac makes her appearance--nor in my opinion will she." He was a little premature. On April 10 the Confederate James River Squadron, led by the *Virginia*, concentrated near Craney Island at the mouth of the Elizabeth River. At daylight the following day, they steamed into Hampton Roads to challenge the Union vessels. Commodore Josiah Tattnall, in command of the Confederate vessels, had expected the *Monitor* to rise to the challenge and attack as soon as his vessels entered the Roads, but the attack did not materialize. Under orders from Goldsborough, Jeffers kept the *Monitor* in the channel near Fort Monroe, with the remainder of the Union fleet beyond, and there she remained. Throughout most of the day the two antagonists steamed back and forth within sight of each other, but neither actually moved within range of the other's guns. Goldsborough wrote to his wife,

> Had the *Merrimac* attacked the *Monitor* where she was and still is stationed by me, I would instantly have been down before the former with all my force . . . .The salvation of McClellan's army, among other things, greatly depends upon my holding the *Merrimac* steadily and securely in check and not allowing her to get past Fort Monroe and so before Yorktown. My game therefore is to remain firmly on the defense unless I can fight on my own terms.

To the *Monitor*'s paymaster, the situation seemed ridiculous.

> Each steamed back and forth before their respective friends till dinner time, each waiting for the other to knock the chip off his shoulder. . . .The same comedy I suppose will be enacted day after day for I don't know how long.

Although Jeffers prophesied a "regular straight out fight" the following day, no attack developed. Tattnall, as he informed his superior, had decided to act "with proper prudence, for with the *Virginia* at the mouth of [the] James River the enemy's operations in that direction may be checked." In short, neither commander had any intention of challenging the other unless there was no chance of failure. Each rightly believed that too much was at stake to risk his ironclad. Keeler felt that Goldsborough was too cautions:

> Capt. Jeffers is a cool, cautious, careful brave man and if he could be allowed a little discretion I honestly believe the Stars and Stripes would now be waving over the *Merrimac* or she would be resting at the bottom of the harbor.

With the *Virginia* apparently checked by the *Monitor*, McClellan's army began moving up the peninsula, using the York River as its line of communication. The *Monitor*'s enforced inactivity frustrated Jeffers. On April 15, he appealed to be allowed to take his vessel up the York River to support McClellan's troops "for a few hours." On April 25, Keeler wrote, "Capt. Jeffers gets almost frantic at times and goes down to see the old Flag (as the Commodore is called) but it does no good."

On Sunday, May 3, Keeler was, as usual, writing his wife when the *Virginia* was sighted. Quarters were sounded and the paymaster, emerging on deck immediately, observed the

> 'Big Thing' as we have nick-named the *Merrimac*. . . just emerging from behind Sewall's [sic] Point, the black cloud from her bituminous coal hovering over her like the genie of evil omen. . . .She steamed over towards Newport News a piece and then came to a stand. . . .Our deck which had been crowded with visitors was speedily vacated--one female who happened to be among the number nearby fainting.

The crew was piped down to dinner. "Capt. Jeffers (who, by the way, loves a good dinner and can tell just how one should be cooked) declaring that as we had tried her before on an empty stomach he would fight her this time on a full one." Once again the anticipated attack did not materialize. The *Virginia*, after remaining in the area for a short while, steamed back into the Elizabeth River.

That night Keeler wrote,

> day after day we remain torpid and inactive. . .tis no fault of our captain you may rest assured--half of his time is spent in contriving plans for crippling or destroying the *Merrrimac*. . . .His plans are no boyish schemes. . . .I honestly believe if his advice had been followed, Norfolk and the *Merrimac* would now be in our possession.

On May 3, General Joseph E. Johnston, in command of Confederate forces defending Richmond and the peninsula, ordered the abandonment of Norfolk. He believed McClellan's advance up that marshy neck of land necessitated this decision. Then two days later, Abraham Lincoln and members of his cabinet paid a surprise visit to Fort Monroe. The president conferred there with Flag Officer Goldsborough and urged the destruction of the *Virginia* and movement up the James River at once.

On the morning of May 8, while the president was still at the fort, a deserter brought information that Norfolk was being evacuated. Lincoln then ordered Goldsborough to bombard Sewell's Point to ascertain whether the Confederates had abandoned the post and to see if the *Virginia* could be drawn out. Six warships, including the *Monitor*, steamed near the point and opened fire. As Keeler described it,

> Capt. J. sent the order to Mr. Gager [pilot] to take her as close in as the water would allow. Then followed a short period of deathlike silence--then an order to Mr. Greene to load with ten second Birney shell (incendiary) then to elevate his tangent sight for four hundred yards--then to take deliberate aim & fire. Bang went the gun, echoed in a few seconds by the exploding shell.
>
> 'Give her the other, Mr. Greene,' & the gun responds. Round goes the turret to bring the ports away from the fort to load which did not take long.
>
> 'Can't you take us in a little closer, Mr. Gager?'
>
> 'I will try sir.'
>
> 'Tell Mr. Greene to lower his tangent to three hundred yards,' & bang, bang, go the guns again--as yet no response from the fort. Their rag still flies but nothing living is to be seen.
>
> We are not within about three hundred yards of the entrenchments & our guns are served as rapidly as possible. . .Capt. J. has left the pilot house & has slid back one of the iron hatches of the turret, stands with his head out to have a good view of the effects of our shot.

The *Virginia* was then in the yard at Portsmouth across from Norfolk, but Tattnall got underway as soon as he heard the bombardment. Shortly after 2:00 P.M., the Confederate warship entered the Roads and stood for the *Monitor*. The Union ironclad was close to the point of shelling Confederate earthworks when her enemy armorclad was observed closing. For a few minutes it looked as if the two ironclads would fight each other again, but it was not to be. Flag Officer Goldsborough signaled to cease firing and "to resume moorings." The Union vessels then slowly retired below Fort Monroe. For her part, the *Virginia* still refused to be drawn into the channel where a number of Union vessels were waiting. Instead she steamed to and fro in the Roads for more than two hours before firing a single shell in defiance and withdrawing back towards Norfolk.

The *Monitor*'s retirement bitterly disappointed many of the *Virginia*'s crew. One of her officers declared, "it was the most cowardly exhibition I have ever seen. . . Goldsborough & Jeffers are two cowards." Jeffers was equally disappointed, and Goldsborough complained to his wife that night, "She [the *Virginia*] kept more in reverse than ever and would not even give me half a chance to run her down." According to Keeler, the *Monitor*'s crew was disillusioned with Jeffers after the May 8 incident. Keeler, who had earlier bragged on Jeffers' determination to bring the *Virginia* to battle and his eagerness for combat, became increasingly critical of him. He later wrote, "We have all been greatly disappointed in our present Capt. He will set at the table and entertain us with plans of the most magnificent conception, but he is most sadly deficient either in ability or power to carry them out."

Jeffers never had another opportunity to fight the *Virginia* because on May 10, she was destroyed by her own crew. The evacuation of Norfolk along with the ironclad's deep draft persuaded her officers that they had no alternative. She was set on fire near Craney Island and early on the morning of May 11, she blew up. A few hours later the *Monitor* steamed past the blackened hulk of her arch-rival on the way to Norfolk.

With the fall of Norfolk and the loss of the *Virginia*, the James River was open. On May 11, Flag Officer Goldsborough ordered the *Monitor*, the ironclad *Galena*, and three wooden vessels to steam up the river toward Richmond. Four days later the Union flotilla arrived at Drewry's Bluff only eight miles from the Confederate capital where obstructions had been placed across the river. The Confederates had blocked the passage with logs and sunken hulks at that point because of its narrowness. To guard the obstructions a series of field fortifications were constructed on the 200-foot bluff high above the river. Seven heavy guns were emplaced there protected by sharpshooters.

As the Union vessels slowly passed up the river within sight of the obstructions, they came under fire from the sharpshooters on both banks. The *Galena* led the way, followed by the *Monitor*, with the three wooden vessels bringing up the rear. Some 600 yards from the obstructions, almost directly beneath the bluffs, the *Galena* dropped her anchor and opened fire. This started a firestorm. She was almost immediately hit by plunging shot and shell from the Confederate batteries above her. Jeffers tried to help by moving the *Monitor* above the *Galena*, but his two guns could not be elevated enough to reach the peaks of the high rock walls. Instead, she had to drop back downstream to a position where her guns could fire over the top of the bluffs. But due to the comparatively long range, the *Monitor*'s fire did little damage to the Confederate defenses. After blazing away for three hours, with the *Galena* badly damaged, the flotilla retired back down the river. The only good that could be said of the fight was that although hit repeatedly, the *Monitor* suffered no damage in the engagement.

Jeffers' ironclad returned to Hampton Roads where she remained idle for most of the summer. The lieutenant, who had only been in command since March 13, wrote to the Navy Department recommending that she be sent to a shipyard for repairs, but the launching of a new ironclad at Richmond delayed her departure. Not until the powerful armored vessel, *New Ironsides*, arrived in the Roads and joined the squadron could the *Monitor* be spared.

On August 15, Keeler informed his wife that Jeffers had been detached from the *Monitor* and "Capt. Stevens of the Maratanza takes his place--I don't know Capt. Stevens, but we can't be any worst off for the exchange." No explanation for his detachment has been located. His pension application suggests that ill health may well have been the reason. This is reinforced by the fleet surgeon who informed the Navy Department on August 2 that the entire flotilla on the James River was in poor physical condition. On August 5, Keeler wrote that he was the "only one on board the ship among the officers and men who has not been oblidged [sic] to take medicine." When Jeffers departed the ship he was a lieutenant commander, having been promoted to that rank on July 16.

Jeffers' health "forbidding further active service," according to his pension application, resulted in his spending the remainder of the war in ordnance work, first at

Philadelphia and, after September 1863, as inspector in charge of experiments at the ordnance yard, Washington Navy Yard. In Philadelphia, Jeffers spent most of his time testing a gunpowder invented by Isaac R. Dillard. Dillard had the backing of Lincoln himself, but the chlorate-based powder was considered too unstable to adopt.

In Washington, among other activities, he assisted in preparing the powder-ship *Louisiana* for explosion on December 24, 1864, off Fort Fisher, North Carolina. Jeffers was one of three naval officers assigned to assist Major General Benjamin Butler, who proposed the idea. Jeffers developed the fuse that was adopted, a mechanism adapted from a marine clock. Unfortunately, the clock-fuse system failed to work and the powder vessel was eventually exploded by fire. This failure had apparently little effect on Jeffers' career, for in March 1865, he was promoted to commander.

With the end of the Civil War, Jeffers' health had apparently improved to the point where he could have sea duty again. He was relieved from ordnance duty and ordered to sea to command the steam sloop-of-war *Swatara*. Jeffers was the *Swatara*'s first captain; he supervised her launching in May and spent the following months getting her ready for service. Assigned to the West India Squadron, she departed from Hampton Roads in January 1866, for Bermuda and the West Indies. For five months she cruised from island to island before returning to the Washington Navy Yard for repairs in May.

The *Swatara* was then assigned to the European Squadron. She steamed out of Norfolk in the middle of June and rendezvoused with the squadron at Lisbon, Portugal, a month later. The first part of the cruise was routine, showing the American flag in various ports in northern Europe. In November she entered the Mediterranean. John Harrison Surrett, one of the conspirators in the Lincoln assassination who had fled to Canada and then to Europe, had been discovered posing as a Zouave in a unit of the Papal army. Rufus King, United States representative to the Papal States, requested that a warship be sent to Civitavecchia to carry Surrett back to the United States. Admiral Goldsborough, in command of the European Squadron at that time, immediately ordered Jeffers to take his vessel to Civitavecchia. Before the *Swatara* reached the Italian coast, Surrett escaped his captors and fled to Alexandria, Egypt, only to be recaptured in a few weeks. The *Swatara* was then sent to Alexandria, where Surrett was carried on board on December 21. Surrett later gave an account of his flight and capture to a newspaper reporter. He said that Jeffers had ordered him "heavily chained and handcuffed," placed in a stateroom and guarded by a marine. On January 8, 1867, the warship with Surrett on board sailed for the United States under strict orders to touch at no port unless absolutely necessary.

The *Swatara* anchored off the Washington Navy Yard on February 18, 1867. The following day a heavily guarded Surrett was rowed to the wharf, where Jeffers surrendered him to a U.S. marshal, backed up by the Washington superintendent of police and a "file of policemen." Surret was, according to one account, dressed in the Zouave uniform. Because of tight security, very few people witnessed the landing of Surrett. Even yard workmen were kept at a distance. Curiously, a number of Indians of the Sioux delegation then in Washington were allowed to witness the event.

By April the *Swatara* was back on station with the European Squadron. In July, Admiral Farragut, who had replaced Goldsborough, ordered the *Swatara* to the eastern Mediterranean under instructions to investigate the possiblity of removing refugees from the island of Crete. A revolution had broken out in Crete and the American diplomatic representative to the Ottoman Empire had urged the evacuation of the refugees. Admiral Farragut was clearly reluctant to use an American warship for this purpose and apparently instructed Jeffers to simply look after American interests. The *Swatara* remained only a brief period on the island. Jeffers reported, "I find that we have no interest whatever in this island, there being no American residents or trade."

In the fall of 1867, Jeffers was detached from command of the *Swatara* and ordered to duty at the Naval Observatory in Washington, D.C. This was followed by a tour in the Navy Department. In July 1870, he was promoted to captain and assigned duty as assistant to the chief of the Brueau of Ordnance. For the remainder of his career, Jeffers would be associated with ordnance.

Jeffers' fascination with ordnance had never abated, even while he was in command of a ship. In 1865 he served on a board of "five leading ordnance experts" to investigate the cause of rupture of large 150-pounder guns in the navy. In 1866 he edited the fourth edition of *Ordnance Instruction for the U.S. Navy*. He would later edit the sixth edition.

As assistant to Commodore A. Ludlow Case, Chief of the Bureau of Ordnance, Jeffers initially concentrated on improving the navy's gunpowder program. The navy purchased the bulk of the gunpowder from the DuPont powder works in Wilmington, Delaware. Jeffers persuaded Case to appoint a naval officer as inspector of powder at the DuPont works and by working closely with him, the power of gunpowder was substantially improved.

In 1871 Jeffers recommended the designation of a vessel as a gunnery-practice ship. In 1858 he had served on the *Plymouth*, the first gunnery-practice ship in the navy. His favorable impressions of that ship, along with the success of the British navy with similar ships, were the major factors in his decision to recommend this. In November, the Secretary of the Navy approved the recommendation, and the famous old frigate *Constellation* was assigned as the gunnery-practice ship. The vessel would be under the Bureau of Ordnance from October until May for the training of seamen in gunnery and under the control of the superintendent of the Naval Academy for the summer midshipmen training cruise. Jeffers took command of the ship. As a gunnery practice ship for seamen, it was not a success. It was unpopular with the seamen who felt, according to one observer, that "too much was attempted." Jeffers, who had the reputation of being a stern disciplinarian, tried to make the frigate into a "crack cruiser," and the crew, with a large percentage of seamen assigned from other ships and stations to temporary duty on the *Constellation*, was unhappy with it. The gunnery-practice ship was discontinued when Jeffers left the vessel in 1873 to become chief of the Bureau of Ordnance.

Jeffers would serve as chief of the ordnance bureau for eight years, or two tours. Along with John Dahlgren, he would have more impact on the development of naval ordnance than any other who held the position of bureau chief. He can, with justification, be called the father of modern ordnance in the U.S. Navy.

Shortly after taking command of the bureau in April 1873, Jeffers pointed out to his superior the relative inferiority of the navy's guns in comparison with those mounted on the warships of many European nations. In his opinion the Dahlgren smoothbores, which had been the standard guns in the navy since 1861, were inadequate to fight modern warships that carried rifled guns. In each of his annual reports from 1874 on, he recommended rearmament of the navy with breech-loading rifled cannon. For most of the period that he was burearu chief, his recommendations concerning naval rearmament were ignored. The 1870s were a period of retrenchment and funds were simply not available. Even if funds had been available, the American iron and steel industry did not have the technological expertise to provide the navy with modern steel guns and Jeffers was opposed to purchasing such weapons abroad. Until steel manufacturers in the United States had developed the necessary expertise and facilities to construct large cannon and until adequate funds were available, Jeffers sanctioned the modification of smoothbores into rifles to improve their firepower and the production of small breech-loading boat guns to demonstrate the soundness of breech loaders. Although the navy would not actually begin rearmament until after he retired, his emphasis prepared the way. As bureau chief, he also worked very closely with steel companies in converting their plants to make the large, high-quality castings and forgings necessary for manufacturing steel breech loaders. Jeffers also placed considerable emphasis on training junior officers as ordnance experts by involving them in experimental projects, publishing their writings, and encouraging them to learn about foreign developments in ordnance.

Richard D. Glasow, in a recent study of the development of modern ordnance in the United States Navy, wrote about Jeffers' contribution:

> Jeffers' foresight and persistence during a so-called period of decay and stagnation resulted in substantial improvement in the quality of domestic gun steel, in knowledge of information about gun design, and in professional expertise that contributed significantly to the resurgence of American naval power during the eighteen eighties. Without the invaluable preparation made by Jeffers and his assistants during the 1870s, the United States Navy could not have rearmed with modern heavy guns so quickly, and the government would not have had a domestic supplier of heavy naval cannon until well after the beginning of the twentieth century.

During these years Jeffers continued writing technical studies concerning naval matters. In 1871 he wrote *Nautical Surveying*, and in 1874, *Care and Preservation of Ammunition*, as well as a number of reports and articles. In 1878 he was promoted to commodore.

Jeffers unfortunately did not live long enough to see the beginning of naval rearmament. After leaving the bureau in 1881, he was ordered to Europe to study developments in ordnance. In 1882 he received orders appointing him to command the Asiatic Squadron, which almost surely would have resulted in his promotion to rear admiral. He was forced to decline the appointment because of a kidney disease. He returned to his home in Washington, D.C., and there died on July 23, 1883, at the age of fifty-nine. Three weeks after his death, a contract was signed for the construction of the first four steel ships in the navy to carry steel breech-loading rifled guns.

Jeffers was a brilliant officer with an inquisitive mind, particularly in technical matters. He was a good seaman and was recognized as "one of the strictest disciplinarians in the service," according to one authority. The only severe criticism of Jeffers came from the pen of the *Monitor*'s paymaster, William Keeler, who a year after leaving the *Monitor* referred to Jeffers as a "brute of a Captain." On the other hand, Keeler occasionally mentioned how entertaining Jeffers was. One insight into this possible contradiction is Keeler's reference to a remark by Jeffers that he had little respect for temporary officers, which would include the paymaster. Keeler may also have reacted to Jeffers' stern discipline for officers as well as enlisted men. S. Dana Greene, Jeffers' executive officer on the *Monitor*, did not criticize his commanding officer and at least one account mentioned Jeffers as a popular officer. Certainly he received high marks so far as his superiors were concerned. There is little doubt that his ability would have carried him to the highest rank in the navy had he lived.

Figure 5. Thomas Holdup Stevens II. (Photograph courtesy of U.S. Naval Historical Center).

THOMAS HOLDUP STEVENS II

Jeffers' successor in command of the *Monitor* was Thomas Holdup Stevens II, son of a distinguished naval officer, Thomas H. Stevens. At the age of eighteen, Stevens, Sr., commanded the *Trippe,* one of Oliver H. Perry's gunboats at the Battle of Lake Erie during the War of 1812. Stevens had as much, if not more, active service than any officer during the Civil War. He participated in combat all the way from the James River in Virginia down the eastern seaboard to Florida, along the Gulf Coast and out into the Atlantic. His name is associated with ships such as the *Monitor* and yacht *America*, battles such as Port Royal and Mobile Bay, and diplomatic incidents such as the *Springbok* case. Finally, like Worden and Selfridge, he would rise to the highest rank in the navy at that time, rear admiral.

Stevens was born May 27, 1819, in Middletown, Connecticut, the son of a naval officer and Elizabeth Read Sage. Young Stevens became something of a pet and protegé of a number of distinguished naval officers of the early years of the navy, such as Thomas McDonough, William Bainbridge, and Charles Stewart, who were friends of his father. Not surprisingly, he was determined to follow his father into naval service. His parents, however, were opposed to this and sent him off to Chicago where he was supposed to learn the profession of banking in a business house belonging to a relative. This parental decision on a career was, as is so often the case, futile, and on December 14, 1836, at the age of seventeen Stevens entered the navy as a midshipman.

His first appointment was to the frigate *Independence*. For the first two years that he served on the *Independence*, she was a unit of the Brazil Squadron, cruising in the South Atlantic. He then spent several months assigned to the Coast Survey before being ordered to the naval school in Philadelphia. He graduated third in his class and on July 1, 1842, was promoted to passed midshipman. He served briefly in 1842 as a naval aide to President John Tyler before being ordered to survey duty in the Gulf of Mexico. For a year he was acting master on the USS *Michigan*, under construction on Lake Erie. The *Michigan* was the navy's first iron-hulled warship. While there he met and married Anna Maria Christie. In September 1844, when the *Michigan* was completed and commissioned, Stevens was ordered to Honolulu in the Hawaiian Islands as naval storekeeper.

United States interests in the Hawaiian Islands became important enough as early as the 1820s to periodically dispatch naval vessels there. The sandlewood trade with China, the South Pacific whaling industry, the presence of American missionaries, along with British interests in the islands, all contributed to the necessity of showing the flag. Shortly after the end of the War of 1812, a Pacific Station was established and the islands came within its responsibility. The vast distance from the United States in the years before we acquired California and the west coast led to the location of a small supply depot in Honolulu. The value of Pearl Harbor as a naval base was unrecognized at this time. Honolulu, although only a small town, was the principal port as well as the capital. Stevens' sojourn in "Paradise" lasted three years. He probably viewed these years with mixed feelings. He was fortunate enough to have his family with him (a daughter, Ellen was born in the islands) and his duty could not have been that taxing, considering the occasional visit by American warships. Yet the Mexican War broke out while he was on Oahu and to a young, ambitious naval officer, it must have been frustrating not to be able to participate in active service on one of the warships engaged in blockade.

However, in February 1847, while the war was still in progress, Stevens was ordered home. Unfortunately, by the time he could engage passage for himself and his family, the Treaty of Guadalupe Hidalgo had been signed, ending the war. To add salt to the wound, as he and his family were returning home in the Chilean ship *Maria Helena* they were wrecked on Christmas Island in January 1848. They were shipwrecked there for more than three months before being rescued. Stevens later wrote a brief account of this ordeal, *Narrative of the Wreck of the Chilean Ship Maria Helena* (1849).

In 1849 he was promoted to lieutenant and ordered back to the *Michigan* on the Great Lakes. The decade of the 1850s was a sequal of duty on various ships, or awaiting orders. After the *Michigan*, he served briefly on the *Germantown* in 1951 before being ordered to the schooner *Ewing*, engaged in survey work on the west coast. He spent nearly five years on this work. In September 1855, Stevens was dropped from the active list of naval officers, apparently at his own request. The most plausible explanation is that he was unable to secure an appointment to a naval vessel and decided to resign his commission. A large number of naval officers did exactly that during this period because of stagnation in the promotion system and not enough billets available for the officer corp.

Stevens remained three years on the inactive list. We do not know how he was employed in what must have been a rather dismal period in his professional life. In January 1858, he was reinstated on the active list and assigned to the *Colorado* in the Home Squadron. In August he was transferred to the frigate *Roanoke* and remained on this warship until 1860. Early in 1861, for the third time in his career, he was ordered to the *Michigan* and was on this ship when the Civil War broke out.

Stevens spent the first weeks of the war on recruiting duty in the Great Lakes area. In September 1861, he was ordered to command the *Ottawa*, a steam gunboat at that time under construction in New York City. One of the class of "ninety day" gunboats, she was commissioned on October 7 and sailed a few days later to join the South Atlantic Blockading Squadron.

Early in November the *Ottawa*, along with her commanding officer, received her baptism of fire. Flag Officer Samuel DuPont had assembled a fleet of thirty-six transports and eleven warships to attack Port Royal, South Carolina. The Union Navy Department had initialed a series of combined operations with the objective of securing designated sites along the southern coast to be used as repair bases and supply depots for the blockading squadrons. Port Royal, with its deep water and situated approximately half-way between the important ports of Charleston and Savannah, was ideally suited as a base. The Confederates, realizing its potential importance, had erected two forts, one on either side of the sound's entrance. Early in the morning on November 7, DuPont's flagship led fourteen vessels, including the *Ottawa,* in two columns steaming up the middle of the channel into the sound. As they came within range of the forts, they opened fire. His heaviest ships, including the *Ottawa*, were to concentrate on the forts while the lighter vessels guarded against an attack by Confederate ships. DuPont's sortee was a complete success. The forts were abandoned after four hours of continuous bombardment by the Union vessels. Stevens, in his report on the action, wrote,

> . . .I weighed anchor, following in the wake of our leading vessel. When abreast of Bay Point battery, finding that our XI-inch gun was giving good execution, I stopped the engine to engage it, and threw about a dozen shells in and about the fortification. . . .About this time a 32-pound shot struck the Ottawa in the port waist. . .wounding severely Mr. Keene, one of the acting masters. . .one other man seriously, and four others slightly, and doing considerable damage to the deck of the vessel

> . . . .Discovering, as we ranged up with the fort on Hilton Head, that we occupied an enfilading position, I continued to occupy it until the enemy deserted their batteries. . . .

It was Stevens, having anchored the *Ottawa* close to the fort on Hilton Head, who reported the Confederate positions abandoned. DuPont then sent an officer to the fort with a flag of truce, and shortly afterwards the Union flag was hoisted over the fort.

Stevens' first battle was over. He had done well and, although his name was not mentioned in DuPont's report of the engagement, there is little doubt that the flag officer was satisfied with his performance.

Port Royal was the first in a rapid series of engagements in which Stevens and the *Ottawa* were involved. He celebrated New Years Day, 1862, by participating in the Battle of Port Royal Ferry. Confederates had concentrated a force of infantry and artillery at a ferry site on the Coosa River, which flowed into Port Royal Sound. Confederate control of the river would prevent Union troops from moving inland to threaten the railroad connecting Charleston and Savannah. It was essential to clear the river and the ferry operation was considered a key point. Two gunboats, including the *Ottawa* and four small boats carrying howitzers, attacked the Confederate positions at the ferry. The gunboats fired on the enemy positions all day while Union troops landed and flanked the Confederate lines. As a result of this combined attack, the Confederates abandoned their positions at the ferry.

Throughout the remainder of January and February, the *Ottawa* was engaged in reconnaissance along the South Carolina coast. Early in March the gunboat was part of a small force that captured Fernandina and St. Mary's, Florida. Because of shallow water, the *Ottawa* was the only vessel to reach Fernandina. As she neared the town, a train was discovered moving along the railway parallel to the water. The *Ottawa* opened fire but the train escaped. The gunboat then steamed up the St. Mary's River and accepted the surrender of the small town with the same name as the river.

Commander Percival Drayton, commanding officer of the expedition, commended Stevens for his action: ". . .had it not been for the constant watchfulness and good management of [Stevens}. . .his vessel would not have been able to. . .enable us to [reach the town without a pilot]."

Stevens had also impressed Flag Officer DuPont. On March 7, only three days after the surrender of St. Mary's, he was ordered to command a force consisting of the *Ottawa*, *Seneca*, *Pembina*, *Isaac Smith*, *Huron*, and *Ellen* and make a reconnaissance of the St. Johns River as far as Jacksonville. He was instructed to temporarily occupy Jacksonville and, with the destruction of all Confederate property, return to Port Royal, leaving one vessel to blockade the river's mouth. They entered the river the following morning. Finding no opposition they proceeded some thirteen miles to Jacksonville, where a deputation surrendered the town. Stevens' men had little property to destroy, as much of it was put to the torch by retreating Confederates. Eight steam sawmills, an iron foundry, ironworking shops, and an unfinished gunboat were destroyed.

Two days after occupying Jacksonville, Stevens reported to DuPont that "I leave this morning [March 12} in the *Ottawa*, with the *Ellen* in company, to penetrate, as far as prudent, the upper waters of the St. Johns." Stevens' disregard of his orders was apparently prompted by news of the yacht *America*, which was supposed to be in hiding somewhere above Jacksonville. In 1851 the schooner *America* became the most famous yacht in United States history by winning a race in the British Isles and beating fourteen of Britain's finest yachts in the process. During the following decade, she raced occasionally and was a pleasure boat for several owners. In 1861 the yacht, renamed the *Camilla*, was used by her British owner to run the blockade out of Savannah, Georgia, carrying on board several Confederate agents. Apparently she was employed as a blockade runner and as such was in the St. John's River when the Union vessels occupied Jacksonville. From a local farmer Stevens learned that the sailing vessel had been scuttled in Dunns Creek about seventy miles from Jacksonville. Stevens' crew raised the *America* in surprisingly short time, plugging her holes, pumping her dry, and then lifting her from the creek bed with large jackscrews. She was then towed to Port Royal and commissioned in the Union navy. DuPont wrote to Assistant Secretary of the Navy Fox, "Stevens with [the *Ottawa*'s]. . . boat and the prize steamer Darlington & Ellen has raised the America. A carpet bag was found containing a letter which gave the precise spot where she had been sunk. . . ."

On March 25, 1862, Stevens was detached from the *Ottawa* and, after a month's leave, ordered to the *Maratanza*, a double-ended wooden steamer of 786 tons. She carried a 9-inch smoothbore and four 24-pounders. In the middle of April the *Maratanza*, under Stevens' command, joined the North Atlantic Blockading Squadron. For more than five months she was almost continuously involved in active service, participating in a number of engagements in the York and James rivers in Virginia. Major General George McClellan had launched his peninsular campaign with the major objective of taking Richmond, the Confederate capital, and the *Maratanza* was one of the units of the North Atlantic Blockading Squadron that cooperated in this campaign. In early May, Confederate troops attacked Union forces occupying West Point on the York River. Stevens, hearing the heavy firing, stationed the *Maratanza* in position to effectively bombard the Confederate positions, and according to army officers present, this gunfire was a major factor in repulsing the attack. A few days later, the vessel steamed into the Pamunkey River and reported no opposition as far as the "White House." This information was passed on to McClellan, who immediately ordered troops to secure the area. The "White House" would later become a military headquarters.

The *Maratanza* was then ordered to the James River. She arrived in the river shortly after a force of Union ironclads, including the *Monitor*, had been repulsed at Drewry's Bluff, a few miles below Richmond. These vessels retired back down the river to await reinforcements. The *Maratanza* was one of the vessels ordered to their support. On May 18, the *Maratanza* and the *Monitor* engaged a small force of Confederate infantry and artillery near City Point, driving them from their positions. On May 30 Stevens' vessel accompanied the *Aroostook* in a sortee up the river to within sight of Drewry's Bluff to determine Confederate strength. Under very heavy fire in which the *Maratanza* was "struck frequently by rifle balls," they retired back down river. The *Maratanza* was then ordered to remain above City Point at a point where a road linked the river with McClellan's advancing army. Flag Officer Goldsborough decided to keep a force of vessels in the vicinity of City Point to guard the army transports supplying McClellan's troops.

On July 4, 1862, the *Maratanza* was instructed to once again make a reconnaissance up the river. Upon nearing Drewry's Bluff, a Confederate gunboat identified as the *Teaser* was discovered. She had apparently been employed in laying torpedoes in the river when surprised by the Union gunboat. Both vessels opened fire. The *Maratanza* was not hit, but the Union gunboat's third shell exploded in the *Teaser*'s boiler. She was abandoned by her crew and Stevens ordered a prize crew aboard to take possession. For this exploit he was later promoted to commander.

On August 9, he was detached from the *Maratanza* and ordered to command the *Monitor*. On August 16 he reported on board to replace William Jeffers. Three days later, Paymaster Keeler wrote his wife, "Commander Stevens. . .has the appearance of a quiet modest man, so far I like him, but I find that first impressions are not always to be trusted. He has the reputation of taking a glass too much occasionally." Stevens would command the *Monitor* less than two months, and Keeler's respect for him would not diminish during this period.

Stevens' tour on the *Monitor* was probably the quietest period of active service during the war for the ironclad. The closest to action that she came was August 28, when the *Monitor* went to the assistance of a tugboat near City Point in the James River under fire from Confederate raiders. Keeler made light of the incident: "The tug imagined she saw some men ashore in a small piece of woods and was letting drive at them." He added, "We couldn't stretch our imaginations quite so far, so concluded to try for something more real and fired half a dozen shell into [a nearby] house, somewhat to the disturbance of woodwork and masonry."

Two days later the *Monitor* was ordered back to Hampton Roads. It was a relief for the *Monitor*'s crew; the ironclad had spent most of the hot summer months up the river. Keeler wrote, "How much pleasanter we find it hear [sic] with the breeze of old ocean sweeping over us, than in the heated furnace like air of James River. . . .For the last three months I have not tread the deck without thinking of what might be in the bushes by our side. . . ." On September 6 he wrote, "the afternoon I spent with Capt. Stevens and our M. D. Fishing, though with rather poor success. . . .Had a very pleasant time with Capt. Stevens. He is good company and a plain pleasant sociable man." Two days later Stevens was detached from the *Monitor* and ordered to command the *Sonoma*. "We parted with him with regret for he had won the respect and esteem of us all," Keeler told his wife.

The *Sonoma* was a new 955-ton side-wheel gunboat launched in April 1862. The success of the Confederate cruisers, especially the *Florida* and *Alabama*, against Union shipping prompted the Navy Department on September 8 to put Commodore Charles Wilkes in command of the West India Squadron, created specifically to seek out and destroy the southern raiders. The *Sonoma* was assigned to this squadron and Stevens, who had impressed the commodore when he commanded the James River Flotilla, was ordered to the gunboat. Wilkes would write in his autobiography that Stevens "was an officer of spirit."

The *Sonoma*, under Stevens' command, was a conspicuous success in the West India Squadron. In the fall of 1862, Wilkes initiated an unofficial blockade of Bermuda, a center of blockade running into the Confederacy. On October 5, the *Sonoma* chased the blockade runner *Harriet Pinckney* back into the port of St. George's, Bermuda, after she had attempted to slip out with a cargo of weapons. On another occasion, Stevens had anchored his vessel just outside the entrance to St. George's when a British warship ordered him to quit blocking the entrance to the harbor. Stevens refused to move his vessel, pointing out that there was enough room for vessels to get by. He also temporarily held up the steamer *Gladiator*, although the merchant vessel was under convoy of H.M.S. *Desparate*. She was allowed to proceed when Stevens was satisfied that the vessel was carrying a legitimate cargo. Both naval vessels cleared for action, but no shots were fired. Throughout all of this, Stevens insisted that he was carrying out the orders of Wilkes, and in fact the flag officer strongly approved of his actions.

The squadron then shifted to the West Indies, with various vessels fanning out in different directions to search for blockade runners. In the middle of January 1863, the *Sonoma* and the *Wachusett* seized the *Virginia* off Mexico. Several additional prizes were taken while the *Sonoma* was under Stevens' command. By far the most important, at least in terms of repercussions, was the British bark *Springbok*. It resulted in a strong protest from the British Foreign Officer and certainly did nothing to improve British-American relations. Nonetheless, the court concluded that she was a legitimate prize.

The *Sonoma* also attempted unsuccessfully to take the Confederate cruiser *Florida* near Nassau. The Union warship chased the Confederate vessel nearly two days before she slipped away during a storm.

In August 1863, Stevens was ordered to command the monitor *Patapsco* in the South Atlantic Blockading Squadron. The *Patapsco* was a veteran ship with a veteran crew, having joined the squadron shortly after her commissioning in January. She had participated in engagements near Savannah and Charleston during the spring and early summer months. Shortly aftrer Stevens assumed command, five monitors, including the *Patapsco*, attacked Fort Sumter. The *Patapsco*'s log stated:

> At 1 a.m. got underway and proceeded toward Fort Sumter. . . .at 2:30 anchored within 800 yards of the forts. At 2:50 opened fire on Fort Sumter. . . .At 6

> a.m. withdrew in obedience to orders from the Adm [Dahlgren]. . .having been engaged three hours and ten minutes.

What this terse statement does not describe was the nearly impossible conditions under which the crew toiled during these three hours, confined in the extremely hot interior of what one of the crew referred to as an "iron coffin."

During the night of September 1, Admiral Dahlgren tried again to bombard Fort Sumter into capitulating. On this occasion the *Patapsco* anchored approximately 500 yards from the fort, and throughout the night, for five hours, she exchanged fire with the Confederate gunners. As before, this attack achieved no apparent success, although Dahlgren commended his monitor commanders, including Stevens, writing that they "handled their vessels with ability in the narrow channel and the obscurity of the night."

Admiral Dahlgren was convinced that Sumter, reduced to rubble by the frequent bombardments, was weakly defended and could be easily captured. He decided to send a landing force to take the fort. Stevens was given the command, and he agreed to take it, although extremely reluctantly, pointing out to the admiral that he knew nothing about conducting an amphibious assault. Dahlgren insisted that he take charge of the mission, saying "you have only to go and take possession. You will find nothing but a corporal's guard."

Stevens later wrote an article on the boat attack on Sumter which was published in *Battles and Leaders of the Civil War*. In it he said that after the conference with Dahlgren, "my convictions of the impracticability of the assault were unshaken. . .but personal appeals [from various officers]. . .had their effect, and I reluctantly consented to go."

Stevens' strong reservations about the attack were proved correct. From the beginning everything went wrong. Union military forces were to cooperate with the sailors and marines in the landing force, but because of a dispute over who would be in charge, they backed out. Five hundred men in small boats were towed near the fort by a tug. When the boats were let go by the tug, they made no effort to coordinate their landing, simply moving to the beach as soon as they could. As the boats reached the shore to disembark their men, they were met by strong resistance. It was clear that the Confederates had knowledge of the planned attack and were waiting for it. In fact, instead of a "corporal's guard," the Confederate force numbered more than 400 men. A few members of the landing party made it to the fort's walls, but were killed or captured. Out of the attacking force, more than 150 were killed, wounded, or captured. The attack was a disaster. Although Paymaster Keeler, when he heard of the attack, wrote his wife that Stevens was "just the person to lead such an expedition," it seems clear that he was not. Although the attack probably had little chance to succeed once it was known to the fort's defenders, Stevens' inexperience was obvious.

Stevens resumed command of the *Patapsco*, more than likely relieved that he was in command of a warship. Admiral Dahlgren, still determined to subdue Charleston through the tactical employment of a naval force, returned to using bombardments to achieve his objective. For forty-one days, starting on October 26, 1863, his ships lobbed shot and shell at the forts defending the port. The *Patapsco* during this period concentrated its fire on the sea face of Fort Sumter. Stevens reported to Dahlgren that during one seven-day period, his vessel fired 455 shells at the fort and 315 hit. He also lost two men when one of his guns burst from the heavy firing. The fort, however, stubbornly held out.

In January 1864, the *Patapsco* was sent to join the naval force off Savannah, Georgia. On February 9 a blockade runner, attempting to slip out through Wassaw Sound, was captured by the monitor. In March, Stevens was detached from the *Patapsco* and ordered "to special duty at New York under Rear Admiral Gregory." This "special duty," which was not defined, lasted less that two months, since on May 27 he was ordered to New Orleans to assume command of the *Oneida*.

The *Oneida* was a screw sloop-of-war that had joined the West Gulf Blockading Squadron under Admiral David G. Farragut shortly after commissioning in February 1862. When Stevens took command, she was attached to the naval force blockading Mobile, Alabama. On July 23 a party of ten men from the *Oneida* carried out a commando raid near Mobile Bay and captured an "entire picket cavalry camp." Five men and their horses were taken, although the animals were later released. Farragut mildly reprimanded Stevens for not killing the horses.

On August 2 Stevens received instructions from Admiral Farragut temporarily detaching him from the *Oneida* in order to take command of the ironclad *Winnebago*, a double-turreted monitor built specifically for operations on the western rivers. She had four XI-inch Dahlgren guns--two per turret--and along with her three sister ships, was the only monitor ever built with triple screws and rudders.

Years after the war Stevens wrote that he had taken the *Winnebago* at the request of Commander J. R. M. Mullany. Farragut was planning to take his fleet into Mobile Bay and expected strong resistance from two powerful forts guarding the entrance and a Confederate naval force, including the ironclad *Tennessee*. The *Winnebago*, under the command of a relatively inexperienced volunteer officer, had recently joined his force, and the admiral had decided to temporarily put a more experienced officer in command. Mullany was available, but he had never commanded an ironclad. Hence he approached Stevens, who had commanded an ironclad and Farragut agreed to the exchange; Mullany would command the *Oneida* and Stevens the *Winnebago* during the operation. Farragut reported that "I ordered Commander Stevens to [the *Winnebago*] . . .for the fight. . . considering that there was too much at risk to trust to the inexperience of a volunteer officer." Stevens later wrote,

> Two or three days before the day appointed for the attack, the present Rear Admiral Mullany then commanding the *Bienville* came on board the *Oneida* . . .with a proposition that I should take the *Winnebago* for the time being and permit him in the attack about to be made to take the *Oneida*, assigning as a reason for the request so urgently made that he had seen but little fighting service. . . .Recognizing the fine spirit prompting the request and being aware from the plan of battle the Admiral had sent to the comdg. officers that in remaining on the *Oneida* I too should be thrown measurably out of the fight I told him if the arrangement he desired was acceptable to the admiral he could say it would be agreeable with me. Mullany shortly after returned with the necessary orders.

August 5 dawned beautiful and cloudless, with ideal conditions for the attacking force. At 5:30 A.M. the fleet got underway in two columns. One of these columns consisted of four monitors with the *Tecumseh* in the lead.

> When the line was fully established I got underway. [the line] steamed. . .between Fort Morgan and the wooden ships [that made up the second column]. Slowly and steadily the Fleet moved on until within easy range when the forts opened their batteries and the Battle had fully begun, the vessels firing as they could bring their guns to bear until all were hotly

> engaged. When near to Fort Morgan feeling apprehensive as we were very close in we might ground upon the spit making off [southwest]. . . from the fort, I walked from the after to the forward turret and ordered the pilot to give the Point a little wider berth. . . .[as] I turned to go again aft to direct the firing of the after guns. . .loud cheering was heard above the din of conflict and I saw nothing of the *Tecumnseh* but the top of the smoke stack and the seathing water beneath which she had gone down.

At approximately 7:30 A.M. the *Tecumseh* struck a mine, reeled to port, and went down within two minutes. The cheering that Stevens heard came from the crews of the flagship *Hartford* and the *Metacomet* as they observed the three remaining monitors steaming unhesitatingly by the sunken *Tecumseh* into the bay. Alfred T. Mahan, in his *Gulf and Inland Waters*, wrote,

> As they passed, the admiration of the officers of the flagship *Metacomet* was aroused by the sight of Commander Stevens, of the *Winnebago*, walking quitetly, giving orders, from turret to turret of his unwieldy vessel, directly under the enemy's guns.

As Farragut's ships entered the bay, they engaged the Confederate warships *Selma, Morgan, Gaines,* and the ironclad *Tennessee*. In the battle that followed, the *Oneida* was seriously damaged by fire from the Confederate ironclad. Commander Mullany lost an arm. Stevens, seeing the *Oneida* in difficulty, conned his monitor between the wooden gunboat and the Confederate ironclad and possibly saved her from destruction. The small Confederate wooden gunboats were captured or destroyed; one escaped back up the bay. The *Tennessee* continued to fight until rammed by three Union warships and, with the *Chickasaw* pounding her mercilessly, the Confederate ironclad surrendered. During this period the *Winnebago* had continued to fire on Fort Morgan. By noon the Battle of Mobile Bay was history and Farragut's fleet was at anchor in the bay.

Farragut, in his report of the battle, wrote,

> The Winnebago was commanded by Commander T. H. Stevens, who volunteered for that positon. His vessel steers very badly, and neither of his turrets will work, which compelled him to turn his vessel every time to get a shot, so that he could not fire very often, but he did the best he could under the circumstances.

On August 18 Stevens left the *Winnebago* to resume command of the *Oneida*. She was then sent to New Orleans for extensive repairs. The vessel remained in the yard for more than six months.

In March 1865, Stevens was ordered to join the blockading force off Texas. For the remainder of the war the *Oneida* was on station in Texas waters. He was present in early June when Confederate generals Kirby Smith and J. Bankhead Magruder surrendered the last southern armies. Captain Benjamin Sands, in command of the naval forces off Galveston, wrote in his memoirs, *From Reefer to Rear Admiral,* "On the morning of June 5th I hoisted my division pennant on the USS Cornubia and crossed the bar at the entrance to Galveston Harbor and in company with Commander Stevens and Downes and

Lieutenant Commander Wilson. . .I landed in Galveston." There they received the surrender of the town.

The Civil War was over. During the hot summer months of 1865, however, the *Oneida* remained in the Gulf. While the American Civil War had been going on, French forces had invaded Mexico. Despite strong protests from the Lincoln government, French occupation forces were not withdrawn. As soon as the war was over, the United States government began strengthening its military and naval forces along the Mexican border and in the Gulf to force the French to withdraw their army. This proved to be successful and the naval force in the Gulf was gradually reduced. In the fall the *Oneida* returned to New York City.

For one whose career during the Civil War was marked by probably more active service than any other officer in the navy, Stevens' postwar career was generally routine. Between 1866 and 1870, he was a lighthouse inspector. In 1867 he was promoted to captain, but despite a request for sea duty, he did not receive command of a ship until August 1870, when he was ordered to the *Guerriere*.

The *Guerriere* was a wooden steam sloop-of-war completed after the Civil War was over. She was under orders to join the European Squadron, but before sailing a sad task had to be performed. In August Admiral Farragut died and it was decided to give him a public funeral in New York City. The *Guerriere* was sent to transport the body from Portsmouth, New Hampshire, where he had died, to New York. Shortly after departing from Portsmouth the *Guerriere* ran aground and the embarrassed Stevens had Farragut's remains transferred to a merchant vessel to be carried on to New York City. The *Guerriere* freed herself in time for the funeral, however. In this way Stevens gave his final service to his commander at Mobile Bay.

The *Guerriere* departed New York City on December 17, 1870, for Lisbon and from there into the Mediterranean. On April 7, 1871, she was host to the Bashaw of Tripoili, who inspected the ship and presented Stevens with the anchor of the frigate *Philadelphia*. The anchor had lain on the beach for more than a half-century after the destruction of the frigate in Tripoli Harbor by Captain Stephen Decatur during the Barbary Wars. From Tripoli the sloop cruised to the ports of Egypt, Lebanon, France, and Italy.

The most embarrasing incident of Stevens' career occurred in Italian waters. In July 1871, the *Guerriere* ran aground and was badly damaged before she could be floated free. The European Squadron at that time was divided into two units with Commodore I. R. Mullany in command of the Mediterranean division. Mullany was an old friend of Stevens', the officer who had been responsible for Stevens receiving temporary command of the *Winnebago*. Mullany, who was under orders to return to the United States, did not investigate the accident, but left for England en route to New York. The admiral in command of the European Squadron, Rear Admiral Charles S. Boggs, Jr., ordered Mullany back to the Mediterranean to conduct a court of inquiry concerning the incident. The court of inquiry was convened and Boggs relieved Stevens of his command until it was completed. When the report was made, Stevens was found at fault and suspended from rank and duty for three years. Seven months later, on November 26, 1872, he was reinstated, probably because of his outstanding record. In February 1873, he was promoted to commodore, retroactive to the date when the suspension was lifted.

From 1873 until 1880 he performed various duties at Norfolk, including a tour as commandant of the Navy Yard. In 1879 he was promoted to rear admiral and the following year ordered to command the Pacific Squadron. At that time the small Pacific Squadron was concentrated on the western coast of the United States with occasional cruises to South American waters and the Hawaiian Islands. Nothing of any significance occurrred to mar Stevens' tour, which was his last active command. On May 16, 1881, he struck his flag as commanding officer of the squadron and ten days later was transferred to the retired list. Forty-five years of service in the United States Navy had come to an end.

After retirement Stevens lived in Washington, D.C., occupying much of his time in writing articles and poetry on naval subjects. Many of these were published in the *Army and Navy Journal, The United Service, The Century Magazine, Philadelphia Times*, and *Battles and Leaders of the Civil War*. During these years Stevens became something of an entrepreneur, investing in business activities and acquiring property, including title to a small banana plantation company in Honduras.

He had a large family of three daughters and six sons. The eldest son became a rear admiral and two others were officers in the army and marine corps. Stevens died on May 15, 1896, at the age of seventy-seven.

Stevens once wrote, "Ambition comes in many forms. . .and often. . .assumes the garb of duty." He may well have been reflecting upon himself, for Stevens' superiors and peers lauded him for his "devotion to duty." He was also considered an outstanding officer. Admiral DuPont emphasized that he was "very superior." Rear Admiral Wilkes would say that "his ability as an officer [was] second to none in the Navy. . . .His duties engrossed his whole attention." Others remarked upon his courage; the term "coolness" was frequently used in describing him. Paymaster Keeler wrote that "the short time that [Stevens]. . .has been on board [the *Monitor*] has made our vessel seem like another place, his treatment of his officers and men has been so kind and pleasant." In 1863 Keeler ran into Stevens and wrote his wife afterwards that "He is a very fine man and a good officer." He was a fine man and a good officer.

Figure 6. John Payne Bankhead. (Photograph courtesy of U.S. Naval Historical Center).

JOHN PAYNE BANKHEAD

John Payne Bankhead was born on August 3, 1821, at Fort Johnston, on Charleston Harbor, South Carolina. His father was General James Bankhead, a regular army officer from Virginia, breveted brigadier general in 1847 for valor at the Battle of Vera Cruz during the Mexican War. His mother was Anne Pyne from Charleston, South Carolina. In August 1838, at the age of seventeen, Bankhead entered the navy as a midshipman. He was appointed to the thirty-six-gun frigate *Macedonian*, where he had his first taste of shipboard life. The *Macedonian* at that time was a unit of the West India Squadron, which cruised the Caribbean as a deterrent to pirates.

After two years on the *Macedonian*, Bankhead was ordered to the *Concord*, a sloop-of-war in the Brazil Squadron. On June 28, 1842, she was ordered to proceed to the island of Tristan da Gunha in the South Atlantic, and from there to Madagascar and the east coast of Africa for the protection of American whaling interests. The *Concord* ran aground on a sand bar in October 1842, at the mouth of the Loango River. The ship was abandoned after the captain drowned and the survivors, including Bankhead, were carried by chartered vessel back to the United States. Bankhead then served briefly on the *Independence*, the flagship of the Home Squadron, before being assigned to the naval school in Philadelphia. Upon leaving the school in 1844, he was promoted to passed midshipman.

In 1845, as with so many other officers during these years, Bankhead found himself ordered to the Coast Survey. Before and after the Mexican War, the navy simply had too many officers for the ships in commission. Bankhead was still in the Coast Survey when the Mexican War broke out. In December 1846, he requested an appointment to one of the ships in the Gulf of Mexico. After a short leave, he was ordered to the Home Squadron, which included the naval force blockading the Mexican Gulf ports. Bankhead was apparently assigned to a naval battery cooperating with General Winfield Scott's army at Vera Cruz. In fact, young Bankhead evidently served with his father. Keeler mentioned that "Capt. B. was chief of his [father's] staff." Shortly after the end of the war, the Secretary of the Navy forwarded a copy of a letter to Midshipman Bankhead from his father, "expressing high commendation of conduct of the officers and men comprising the naval battery."

When the war ended, Bankhead took an extended leave of absence, possibly because of illness, and in 1850 reported on board the sloop-of-war *Vandalia* in the Pacific Squadron. Bankhead spent two years on this vessel. On April 7, 1852, he was promoted to lieutenant and shortly afterwards was ordered back to the east coast of the United States. Because of illness Bankhead took leave in 1853. On June 3, he was ordered to report his state of health to the Navy Department each week until he had recovered. In 1854 he had recovered and was assigned to the sailing frigate *Columbia*, flagship of the Home Squadron. In 1855 the frigate was placed in ordinary and Bankhead was assigned to the *Constellation*. This old ship had been laid down in 1794 and commissioned as a frigate. In 1845, after nearly a half-century of sailing throughout the world, she was decommissioned. In 1855 she was brought out of ordinary and recommissioned as a twenty-two-gun sloop-of-war after extensive modifications. The *Constellation* carrying the flag of Commodore Charles Bell, sailed for a three-year tour with the Mediterranean Squadron. In 1858 she returned and Bankhead was once again sent to the Coast Survey, this time in command of the small schooner *Cranford*. He was still on this duty when the Civil War broke out.

Bankhead was from prominent families in both Virginia and South Carolina. As with so many other families, secession and the conflict that followed badly divided his family. John Bankhead had two brothers, Henry C., a regular army officer who also remained loyal to the flag, and Smith Pyne, a lawyer in Memphis, Tennessee, who joined the Confederate army and became a colonel. Major General John Bankhead Magruder was a cousin. We have no idea what kind of pressure John Bankhead was under to resign his commission and follow his state as so many other southern naval officers did. We have no record of any thoughts that he had on this. We do know that both his mother and father had died, that he considered New York to be "home," and, like a few southerners such as David Farragut and Percival Drayton, he retained his commission in the United States Navy.

After the firing on Fort Sumter and the declaration of a blockade, Bankhead was ordered to the *Susquahanna*, a side-wheel steamer carrying fifteen guns launched in 1850. She had been on the Mediterranean station when the war broke out and sailed for the United States immediately after the news of Fort Sumter. She reached Boston in May, and after a period of refit, joined the Atlantic Blockading Squadron. In August the *Susquahanna* participated in the joint army-navy expedition to Hatteras, North Carolina. On August 28 the Union naval force, including the *Susquahanna*, bombarded the forts guarding Hatteras Inlet as troops landed. The following day the bombardment continued until the forts surrendered. Bankhead later wrote Captain Gustavus Fox, the Assistant Secretary of the Navy and an old shipmate,

> . . .without wishing to comment too critically upon the acts of my superior, I can't help thinking that the whole business was very loosely managed. Had a boat been sent in to take soundings and a few buoys placed at the commencement of shoal waters, the squadron could have gone in close and finished the whole matter up in a few hours instead of two days and saved to the Government money, tons of shot and shell which were literally thrown away and produced no effect whatever (except noise). Hatteras is perfectly secure at present against any force. . .our services may well be disposed with here and made available farther down the coast.

On September 29, a few days after writing the above, the armed tug *Fanny* was taken by Confederates while carrying provisions to Union troops stationed at the north end of Hatteras Island. Bankhead was put in command of armed launches and instructed to protect the small boats carrying provisions to those troops. On October 8 he was ordered to New York to take command of the screw gunboat *Pembina*, one of the "ninety day gunboats" recently launched at the Novelty Iron Works.

Earlier Bankhead had written to Assistant Secretary Fox, pointing out that he "was two and a half years surveying on the coast [of South Carolina and Georgia] and perfectly conversant with it. . . .Should an opportunity present itself and a Lieut. commanding may be wanted I hope you will bear me in mind." Apparently Fox did "bear [him] in mind," for almost immediately after the letter reached Washington, Bankhead was ordered to the *Pembina*.

On November 5 the *Pembina* joined the South Atlantic Blockading Squadron assembled off the South Carolina coast to attack Confederate defenses at Port Royal Sound. The *Pembina*, along with other warships including the *Ottawa* under later USS *Monitor* captain Stevens, engaged and dispersed a small Confederate naval force in Port Royal Sound, then joined in the bombardment of the forts guarding the entrance to the sound. Bankhead, in his report on the bombardment, said that he commenced firing at 10:15 A.M. and ceased at 2:15 P.M. when the enemy was discovered leaving the battery.

After the occupation of the forts by Union troops, the large vessels dispersed for blockade duties and the lighter ones, including the *Pembina*, began to probe the inland waters and small harbors in the vicinity of Port Royal. The *Pembina* and two other vessels examined Beaufort harbor. On November 11 Flag Officer Samuel DuPont was informed that Beaufort was under Union control and "the pillage has ceased, owing to the judicious measures instituted by lieutenant Bankhead and Watmough."

From Beaufort these vessels made a reconnaissance of St. Helena Sound and the Coosaw River. The *Pembina*'s log reported on November 25, "in St. Helena Sound and Coosaw River. . .At 3:30 fired the rifled [gun] and the XI-inch gun at a fort on Sams Point." November 26: "at 6:40 a.m. gig and first cutter ashore; crews engaged in destroying ordnance in Fort Heyward, Sams Point, S.C." November 27: "at 6:30 a.m. followed the steamer *Vixen* up the Ashpoo River, South Carolina. . . .at 7 fired shell and rifled gun at a fort on the northeast bank of the river."

In December 1861, the *Pembina* accompanied the "light" gunboats *Ottawa* and *Seneca* to Wassaw Sound, Georgia, on a reconnaissance. Finding no fortifications, the vessels steamed to Ossabow Sound and up the Vernon River, where they discovered a fort. No effort was made to attack the fortification and only one shot was fired at the vessels as they withdrew. On December 18 Bankhead was ordered to return to Wassaw Sound because of information received that the blockade runner *Fingal* was going to try and slip out. The *Pembina* was still on station there at Christmas but departed for Port Royal three days later. As they discovered afterwards, the Confederates decided to convert the *Fingal* into an ironclad, the *Atlanta*.

On January 1, 1862, the *Pembina* was one of a small force of gunboats that attacked Confederate positions at Port Royal Ferry on the Coosa River (see Stevens' account of this action.) Bankhead's vessel then rejoined the blockading force off Savannah. Flag Officer DuPont and General Thomas W. Sherman, in command of Union troops cooperating with the naval force in the South Atlantic, planned to use the gunboats stationed in Wassaw Sound as a diversion for an attack on Fernandina, Florida. On January 27, Commander John Rodgers with three vessels, including the *Pembina*, ascended Freeborn's Cut, southwest of the Savannah River. Confederate officers were convinced that an attack on Fort Pulaski was imminent. The Confederate naval commander in Savannah, Josiah Tattnall, steamed down the Savannah River with a force of wooden gunboats and exchanged gunfire with Rodger's vessels, but no vessel on either side was hit. Rodgers withdrew his ships out of range.

The *Pembina* remained in the vicinity of Watt's Cut to protect troops as General Sherman established control of the water approaches to Savannah. Throughout this period, Bankhead's experience in surveying was utilized to mark channels and entrances. In February, while marking a channel in Wright's River near its entrance to the Savannah River, his surveying party came under fire. Ignoring this, Bankhead's men continued their work and discovered a line of torpedoes anchored across the river "in the channel."

In March the *Pembina* was ordered to participate in the attack on Fernandina, Florida. Bankhead's vessel never made it to Fernandina, running aground along with several other vessels in the flotilla approximately three miles from the town. It was the *Ottawa*, under Lieutenant Stevens, that reached Ferandina and accepted its surrender. The *Pembina* was also with the *Ottawa* in the expedition up the St. Johns River to Jacksonville. When Stevens withdrew his small naval force, he left Bankhead in the *Pembina* at Mayport to blockade the river.

On May 15 Bankhead was ordered to join the blockading force off Charleston. The *Pembina* was assigned to this important blockading station because of her shallow draft, which was necessary for inshore duty. The flag officer commanding the South Atlantic Blockading Squadron wanted to secure control of the Stono River, and because of the river's depth a shallow-draft vessel was needed. The *Pembina* arrived off Charleston on

May 16 and Bankhead was ordered by the senior officer present, Commander John B. Marchand, to determine if the water over the bar at the entrance to the Stono River was deep enough to allow his warships to cross over. Commander Marchand recorded in his journal that night: "At nine, several boats were sent to sound the bar, but I in my gig, and Lieut. Bankhead. . .in his, pulled across the shoal and entered the Inlet. Lieutenant Bankhead was more particularly engaged sounding whilst, in my gig, I pulled ahead reconnoitereing [sic]. . . ." He came under rifle fire and fell back while Bankhead completed the soundings. The water was too low for the gunboats to cross but Bankhead was instructed to keep the *Pembina* as close to the inlet as possible and to cross at "the first opportunity." On May 20 three gunboats, including the *Pembina*, were able to get over the bar into the river. They immediately opened fire on a fort on Cole's Island, and began to move slowly up the river, firing at nearby buildings as they went. On the following day they continued probing the river. On May 29 a Confederate steamer was observed rounding a bend approximately a mile up the river from the Union vessels. Marchand wrote in his diary that

> [Commander Percival Drayton] hesitated about going after her as a contraband from the wharf at. . . Grimball's [Plantation] haled [sic] the *Ottawa* in passing, and reported that torpedoes had been placed in the river. . . .However, daredevil Bankhead. . . obtained permission to pull in the gig about a mile up to where there was a bend in the river to take a look.

He reported that the Confederate vessel had passed on up the river around another bend and out of range.

Throughout the summer of 1862, Bankhead remained on blockade duty near Charleston. He must have had mixed feelings about this. His mother was from Charleston, he had been born there, and had spent much of his youth there. Horatio L. Wait, one of the *Pembina*'s officers, later wrote in an article that

> . . .up to the outbreak of the war [Bankhead] . . .had been an especial favorite in Charleston society, and particularly so with a Miss _____. At the first opportunity after the blockading fleet appeared off Charleston, this lady gave one of her slaves his freedom, and sent him to Commander Bankhead, with an elegant set of silver coffin-handles, and a grandiloquent message to the effect that the Coffin to which they belonged was ready and waiting in Charleston. Bankhead had the glistening handles put up on the dark walnut panel over the cabin transom, attracting attention and causing many enquiries, which the waggish recipient seemed to enjoy answering.

Charles A. Post, who served with Bankhead on the *Florida*, confirmed this incident in "A Diary on the Blockade in 1863." He said that the lady was Bankhead's cousin and added,

> Suppose that we had captured the lady! To any one who has ever met Mrs. X and my gallant and courtly commander, the mere suggestion of the situation is delightful. The sparks which would have flown

from the polished rapiers of their wit would have
illuminated this diary, and made it a classic.

By the middle of August, the *Pembina* was in serious need of repairs and on August 22 Bankhead was ordered to take her to New York City. In giving Bankhead his orders, Flag Officer DuPont wrote,

> I take this occasion to say that you have shown yourself a very efficient commanding officer in this Squadron. I have always been gratified at the very prompt manner, however short the notice, in which you were always ready for service, and the fidility [sic] with which you executed my orders. This, with the excellent discipline of your vessel, and her good order, have left nothing to desire in the *Pembina*. . .I shall be much pleased to have you return to this Squadron.

An impressive compliment and DuPont meant it. He wrote to Fox that "of [the *Pembina*'s]. . .commanding officer it is my duty to say that he. . .is a superior officer-- very prompt, crew in fine discipline, vessel less out of order in the months than any other . . . .He has certainly shown himself competent as a Commander." Finally, DuPont wrote, "He wants an iron vessel."

Fox granted him this wish. Upon arriving in New York, Bankhead received orders to take command of the *Monitor*. He arrived at Hampton Roads and relieved Stevens on September 10. Shortly after the change of command, a board of survey condemned the ironclad's engines and boilers and recommended that they be extensively overhauled. Bankhead was instructed to take the vessel to the Washington Navy Yard as soon as the *New Ironsides* arrived. On September 30 the *Monitor* got underway, under tow of a small tug, and by daylight the following day entered the Potomac. She arrived in Washington on October 3 and was placed in drydock. Bankhead departed for three weeks' leave.

From the 1850s throughout the Civil War, Bankhead notified the Navy Department that his mailing address when on leave was a hotel in New York City. With the death of his parents in 1856 and the alienation of his family ties in Virginia and South Carolina as a result of the war, he apparently had no place that he could call home. He once told Paymaster Keeler,

> Well Purser, . . .I think you and me will have to depend on the rest for our good things--I have neither mother, wife or sister to send me such things [packages of food, etc.] but I hope some of my New York friends will send me some good wine and cigars.

Although forty-one years old in 1862, he was still a bachelor.

For nearly six weeks the ship would remain in the capital while her bottom was scraped, the entire vessel cleaned and painted, engines and boilers overhauled, and a number of improvements made. She was taken out of drydock on October 26 to receive more than mechanical attention.

The *Monitor* was a popular attraction to the people in the Washington area. Crowds lined the Potomac River's banks as she was towed into the yard. President Lincoln paid a visit to the ship shortly after she was taken out of drydock, and was received in a formal ceremony. On November 6, the ironclad was open to the public. Long before daybreak folks queued up at the navy yard and climbed on board in droves. Wrote the assistant paymaster,

> Our decks were covered and our ward room filled with ladies & and on going into my state room I found a party of the 'dear delightful creatures' making their toilet before my glass, using my combs & brushes. . . .There appeared to be a general turn out of the sex in the city. . .an extensive display of lower extremities was made going up & down our steep ladders.

"Bully for the *Monitor*!" exclaimed the *Washington Star* . But this pleasant diversion was all too brief, and within two weeks the refitted vessel had joined the fleet in Hampton Roads.

Back in its familiar surroundings and anchored off Fort Monroe, the ship gradually settled down into a state of inactivity. Routine work was carried out, additional improvements made, construction started on an iron shield to go around the top of the turret, and living conditions were much improved over the previous summer in the Roads. The only exception was constant water seepage that caused dampness to prevail in the officers' and crew's quarters.

On Christmas Eve, 1862, the *Monitor* received orders to move to Beaufort, North Carolina. From there she was to join a blockade squadron off Wilmington or Charleston. The paddle-wheel steamer *Rhode Island* received orders to tow the *Monitor* and on Christmas Day the ironclad made ready for sea. Many of the same preparations were made as on the first voyage from New York. "The turret and sightholes were caulked, and every possible entrance for water made secure, only the smallest openings being left in the turret top and the blower stacks through which the ship was ventilated." The turret was wedged up from its center post and oakum was stuffed around its circumference as a seal. The helm was moved from the pilot house to the top of the turret because the forward section was frequently awash when under way and in heavy weather. Finally, stores, powder, and ammunition were taken on board.

Bad weather delayed her departure until December 29. At noon two hawsers were passed from the *Rhode Island* to the *Monitor*. Shortly after 2:00 P.M., she left Hampton Roads for the last time. At 4:45 the *Rhode Island* dropped the pilot off at Cape Henry, and slowly towed the ironclad out into the hungry waters of the Atlantic.

The first twenty-four hours at sea were uneventful. The water was smooth and the weather moderate for that time of year. The crew, however, had difficulty sleeping that night. With the deck light openings secured, the air below deck rapidly became stale. And although dawn, December 30, brought continued good weather, Commander Bankhead later reported that they began "to experience a swell from the southward, with a slight increase of the wind from the Southwest, the sea breaking over the pilot-house forward and striking the base of the 'tower'. . .forcing men to leave the deck for shelter on top of the turret."

By noon the ships, steaming at four to six knots, had gone more than 100 miles and were skirting North Carolina's outer banks. By one o'clock Cape Hatteras lighthouse, some fourteen miles distant, was in sight. During the afternoon the weather steadily worsened, the wind continued to increase in velocity, and the seas in violence. Crew members who ventured above deck had to huddle on top of the turret as the *Monitor* 's flat deck was continually awash.

Seaman Francis Butts, who had enlisted while the vessel was in Washington, later wrote,

> The vessel was making very heavy weather, riding one wave, plunging through the next as if shooting straight for the bottom of the ocean, splashing down on another with such force that the hull would tremble with a shock that would sometimes almost take us off our feet, while a fourth would leap upon us and break far above the turret.

Very little water, however, was taken on board, and the bilge pumps were able to take care of the water that did find its way below.

Late in the afternoon the sea abated somewhat and the officers, except those on watch, sat down to dinner. Although the water was rolling over their heads and crashing into the turret, according to one of the officers present, they laughed, joked, and carried on normal conversation. At nightfall the *Monitor* was directly off Cape Hatteras where the seas were notoriously dangerous. Then between seven and eight o'clock the situation grew grim. One of the hawsers broke and the ironclad began to yaw and tow badly. As the waves rolled across the deck, completely submerging the pilot house before pounding into the turret with great force, the ship began to take on more and more water. The captain was informed that water was seeping into the coal bunkers. Bankhead immediately realized the seriousness of the news. Steam pressure had to be maintained in order to keep the pumps going. Wet coal could not keep the pressure up sufficiently. So pressure began to drop, and by eight o'clock it was down to twenty pounds, far below what was adequate to work the pumps. Within an hour, more than an inch of dirty water was sloshing around in the engine room and rising steadily.

By ten o'clock the ships were barely making headway against gale force winds howling out of the south and southwest. Heavy rain, at times traveling horizontally, reduced visibility until the *Monitor* could hardly be seen from the *Rhode Island*. A *Harper's Weekly* correspondent later described the scene from the paddle wheeler:

> The storm was at its height, the waves striking and passing over the *Monitor*, burying her completely for an instant, while for a few seconds nothing could be seen of her from the *Rhode Island* but the upper part of her turret, surrounded by foam.

Shortly after ten o'clock the engineer reported more than a foot of water in the engine room and getting close to the fire boxes. It was clear to Commander Bankhead that the vessel could not be saved. After a consultation with the officers, a red lantern was raised above the turret, a prearranged signal of distress. The crew worked feverishly to keep the wallowing ironclad afloat until the *Rhode Island* could provide assistance. Gangs were organized to bail the water out; the final hawser was cut by three volunteers who crossed the water-swept deck to sever it. One of the volunteers was lost overboard.

At 11:30 P.M. Bankhead ordered the engines stopped and the anchor dropped. Seaman Butts was ordered to go below and check on the water depth. "I went forward," Butts wrote, "and saw the water running in through the hawse pipe, an eight inch hole, in full force, as in dropping the anchor and cable had torn away the packing that had kept this place tight." Only a few minutes after reporting back to the captain, he was ordered to check the level again:

> I was again sent to examine the water in the wardroom, which I found to be more than two feet above the deck; and I think I was the last person who saw Engineer G. H. Lewis as he lay seasick in his bunk, apparently watching the water as it grew

69

> deeper and deeper, and aware what his fate must be
> . . . .As I ascended the turret-ladder the sea broke
> over the ship, and came pouring down the hatchway
> with so much force that it took me off my feet, and at
> the same time the steam broke from the boiler-room
> as the water has reached the fires, and for an instance
> I seemed to realize that we had gone down. Our fires
> were out and I heard the water blowing out of the
> boilers.

Commander Bankhead prepared to abandon ship. Distress flares were repeatedly sent up. Paymaster Keeler later attempted to describe the feelings of the crew during the time that they anxiously waited for sight of the *Rhode Island*'s boats:

> Words cannot depict the agony of those moments as
> our little company gathered on the top of the turret,
> stood with a mass of sinking iron beneath them,
> gazing through the dim light over the raging waters
> with an anxiety amounting almost to agony for some
> evidence of succor from the only source to which we
> could look for relief.

Finally they observed lifeboats approaching. The first boat reached the *Monitor* and was nearly crushed against the ironclad's side before sixteen men could tumble in. A second lifeboat came alongside and began loading up. Crew members "descended from the turret to the deck with mingled fear and hope," the *Monitor*'s surgeon later wrote.

> Some were washed over as they left the turret, and
> with a vain clutch at the iron deck, a wild throwing
> up of the arms, went down. . . .A sailor would
> spring from the deck to reach [the boat]. . .be seen
> for a moment in mid-air, and then, as she rose, fall
> into her.

About twenty-five to thirty men remained on board the sinking vessel. Two boats from the *Rhode Island* made the hazardous trip across to the storm-tossed ironclad, using the red lantern to guide them through the gloom. Commander Bankhead ordered all hands into the approaching boats. "Some were able to jump into the boats, and some landed in the water and were hauled in," a member of one of the boat crews later wrote. The two boats quickly filled up with members of the *Monitor*'s crew, including the captain, but two or three, paralyzed by fear, refused Bankhead's plea to jump. The two boats then made the difficult journey back to the *Rhode Island*.

The *Rhode Island*'s boats desperately tried to rescue those remaining on the *Monitor*, but to no avail. One boat disappeared and was not found until the following day. At approximately 1:00 A.M., December 31, the men lining the *Rhode Island*'s rail saw the ironclad's red and white lights hanging above her turret disappear. "The *Monitor* is no more," wrote Paymaster Keeler.

Bankhead suffered from exposure and after being rescued by the *Rhode Island* was sent to New York City on sick leave. Shortly after arriving in New York, he was ordered to take command of the *Florida*, at that time under conversion at the Brooklyn Navy Yard. The *Florida* was a side-wheel vessel of about 1,200 tons employed in the prewar years as a merchant steamer on the New York to Savannah run. When commissioned she carried a battery of four 9-inch smoothbores on her spar deck, a 100-pounder Parrot in the waist, and a 50-pounder Dahlgren on the topgallant forecastle. Because of her speed, heavy battery and comfortable quarters, she was considered a good command and most suitable for blockade service.

During the winter months of 1863, Bankhead made an occasional visit to the yard to check on the ship's progress, but his "severe indisposition," as he described his illness to the Secretary of the Navy, kept him convalescing most of the time. He was apparently still not completely well when the *Florida* was commissioned on March 7. Assistant Secretary Fox had already informed Flag Officer Samuel P. Lee, in command of the North Atlantic Blockading Squadron, that the *Florida* would be assigned to him for blockade duty.

On March 9, the *Florida* got underway with the new monitor *Nantucket* in tow. Bankhead's clerk remarked in his diary, "It is strange that [Bankhead's]. . . .next job should be to tow a monitor over the old ground. I fancy that he prefers the role of tower to that of towee." Keeler, who had joined the *Florida* as her paymaster at Bankhead's request, wrote his wife that night as they rounded Sandy Hook, "This is the anniversary of our fight with the *Merrimac*."

On March 15, after a week of towing the *Nantucket* south through heavy weather, they reached Port Royal. From there the *Florida* returned to Hampton Roads, and after Bankhead met with Flag Officer Lee, she steamed to her assigned station on the Wilmington blockade, the most difficult duty in the North Atlantic Blockading Squadron. On March 28, Keeler wrote in some despair, "Here we are Dear Anna, on 'Our Station,' and here we are like to be for I don't know how long. . . .It is to be one full monotonous round, day after day, week after week, yes and month after month. . ." The captain's clerk mentioned in his diary, "Our duties have fairly begun. . .at night the ship is required to be kept in the most perfect silence. No lights of any kind are shown. It reminds one of a great hunt, the way we lie, waiting for our game." The "game," of course, were the blockade runners, attempting to slip in or out of the Cape Fear River past the *Florida* and other Union vessels.

In the five months that Bankhead commanded the *Florida*, she remained off Wilmington nearly all the time, with occasional trips to Beaufort, North Carolina, for minor repairs, to take on coal and stores, and liberty for the crew. The fervent hope of every blockader was to capture a blockade runner. The *Florida* caught her first one on June 11. In order to break the tedium of blockade duty and its depressing monotony, or as Keeler said,

> Tired of. . .killing time, we started off yesterday morning on a fishing excursion. . . . We had splendid luck catching hundreds of the finest blackfish until 3 o'clock P.M. when tired of the sport we were just getting up our anchor to return to the fleet when 'sail ho' from the look out would have started us all into activity, had it not been so many times repeated and we been so often fooled in chase of one of our own vessels.

In this case it was a blockade runner and after a three-hour chase, the runner hove to. As the *Florida* neared the other vessel, crew members could be observed dumping things overboard. Bankhead's clerk wrote in his diary that night, "'Train the two pivots on her,' said the Captain. He then ran out on the guard and hailing them said: 'throw one more thing of any kind overboard and I'll send a broadside into you,. . . .if you attempt to scuttle the ship, or blow her up, you can take care of yourselves. I shan't pick up a single man.'" Bankhead then sent a prize crew on board the vessel, which proved to be the *Calypso* of 800 tons.

Just a week after taking the *Calypso*, the *Florida* hit the jackpot again. The schooner *Hattie*, carrying 500 barrels of turpentine, 100 barrels of rosin and 50 bales of cotton, was made a prize.

> We feel quite excited at this last capture. . . .How sore (the other blockaders) . . .will feel when they hear of it. Some of them have been down here over eighteen months and have not made a capture for the want of judgement and energy on the part of the commanding officer. They will lie at anchor day after day without attempting to give chase to Strange sails that are often reported. Not so Capt. Bankhead. No sooner comes our anchor (if it is down for we lie a good deal of the time floating around, not coming to anchor), off we go flying the Signal, 'a strange sail in sight,' not waiting for orders to give chase. If Capt. B. had the control of matters on the blockade, things would be hurried up some I assure [you]. There would be less writing done & but little regard paid to red tape but the blockade would be far more effective. He is untiring, up day & night. When he does sleep, it is usually during the day & in clothes. No one knows when he will be on deck during the night & woe betide the one found wanting when he does come.

The *Hattie* was the *Florida*'s last capture under Bankhead. In early August, the *Florida* went to Beaufort to refill her bunkers with coal and while there Bankhead became seriously ill. He was taken to Morehead City, across the bay from Beaufort, and quartered in a small house. There he remained under a doctor's care until well enough to be transported north. Keeler wrote that Bankhead "was taken severely sick again with inflamation of the bowels." Years later, Bankhead's clerk on the *Florida*, in writing an introduction to his diary for publication, said, "In light of what I know now, Captain Bankhead undoubtedly had an attack of appendicitis and subsequently died from the same disease." Shortly after the *Florida* arrived in Beaufort, Bankhead himself wrote Assistant Secretary Fox "begging that I might be ordered out of the old Broken down *Florida* & to one of the new double enders." On August 3 he wrote to Captain Henry Wise, Chief of the Bureau of Ordnance, that he was "a little shaken. . .[but] a few days rest [will]. . .do me good."

Bankhead was transported by merchant vessel to New York City and as before took up residence in a hotel while recuperating. On September 6 he wrote the Department that he had "had [a] relapse of my former illness, since my arrival north." Three weeks later he wrote that he was confined to bed with very little improvement.

During the fall and early winter months of 1863-1864, he recovered slowly. In January 1864, he requested active duty and on February 3 was assigned to command the new double ender side-wheel gunboat *Otsego*. She was commissioned in the spring and reached Hampton Roads May 24, 1864. The *Otsego* was assigned to the North Atlantic Blockading Squadron with her station to be the North Carolina sounds. On June 21 Bankhead was given command of Union naval forces in the sounds. His major responsibility was the Confederate ironclad ram *Albemarle* up the Roanoke River. In April Confederate troops assisted by the *Albemarle* had taken Plymouth, North Carolina, a few miles up the Roanoke. On May 5 the *Albemarle* descended the river and attacked Union gunboats in the sound in an engagement that lasted nearly three hours. The Confederate vessel, damaged, returned to Plymouth. Throughout the summer months it was feared that she would again attempt to enter the sounds and Bankhead, with the *Otsego* and four additional gunboats, guarded the river's mouth. Sometime in the late summer or early fall, he was detached from the *Otsego*, probably because of poor health.

Early in 1865 he was given command of the steam sloop-of-war *Wyoming*, carrying a battery of six heavy guns. The *Wyoming* had spent much of 1864 searching for Confederate cruisers throughout the world. During the fall and winter months, she was in a shipyard at Philadelphia for a complete overhaul. On April 11, 1865, the *Wyoming* was recommissioned with orders to proceed to the East India station.

Secretary of the Navy Welles, in his orders to Bankhead on March 27, wrote,

> Recent intelligence advises us of the arrival of the rebel steamer *Shenendoah* at Melbourne, Australia, and it is believed that she will make the straits and passes to China the field of her piratical operations. Your chief and first object will be the pursuit and (should you be so fortunate as to overtake her) the capture or destruction of the *Shenendoah*. Hence you are expected and directed to follow her whereever she may go. . . .

The war was over before the *Wyoming* arrived in Asian waters. Bankhead informed the Department of his arrival at the Cape of Good Hope on August 11, and at Singapore on September 25. By then the elusive *Shenandoah*, disguised as a British merchant vessel, was well on her way toward Cape Horn and back to Great Britain.

The *Wyoming* remained in Asian waters after the search for the *Shenandoah* ended. She became a unit of the Asiatic Squadron when that squadron was established in 1867. In February 1866 Rear Admiral Henry H. Bell, in command of the station, ordered the *Wyoming* to cruise along the China coast to the open ports of Amoy, Foochow, Ningpo, and Shanghai. Noting the recent reports of increasing piracy, he was to "pursue the pirates with vigor, destroy their vessels, and deliver the men you may capture to the mandarin through the agency of the U.S. Consul for punishment."

On February 21 the *Wyoming* got underway for what proved to be a three-month cruise on the China coast. No pirates were encountered and the only incident to disrupt an otherwise routine voyage was when the ship struck a submerged rock in a dense fog. Although leaking heavily from the damage, she was able to limp into Foochow for docking and repairs.

On July 25, 1866, Bankhead was promoted to captain, but he unfortunately was able to enjoy this promotion less than a year. His health began to deteriorate once again, and early in 1867 he was forced to ask to be relieved of the *Wyoming*'s command. On April 27, 1867, he died near Aden, Arabia, on the steamer that was taking him home.

Bankhead was only forty-six years old when he died, but more than half of his life had been spent in the navy. Considering his professional accomplishments and the respect of his superiors that was apparent, it seems almost certain that, had he lived, he would have become a rear admiral, the highest rank in the navy in postwar years.

Bankhead, as with many regular officers, had a healthy suspicion of politicians. Unlike most officers, however, he had no hesitation about speaking his piece in public, at times to the discomfort of his superiors. Keeler mentioned in a letter to his wife on September 14, 1862, that "we were discussing the probability of the next Presidency at the breakfast table this morning when Capt. Bankhead . . .said, 'McClellan will never be President, he is too high minded and honorable a man to mix up with the dirty, dishonest politicians in the Captial.' " In December he wrote, "[Bankhead] is 'down' on the politicians who he claims are attempting to control the movements of our armies, he denounces them most bitterly attributing to them most of our reverses." Secretary of the Treasury Salmon P. Chase remarked in his diary that Bankhead had told one of his assistants that "the Gov't ought to be superceded by McClellan." Chase made a point of passing on Bankhead's remark to Secretary of the Navy Welles, who requested that Chase's assistant put it in writing. When this was done Welles confided in his diary that Bankhead's statement was "less strong perhaps in words but about as offensive." Not surprisingly, Welles called the attention of his assistant, Fox, to Bankhead's unfortunate remark. Fox, of course, tried to smooth over his friend's "indiscretion," which entailed, as he informed Flag Officer Lee, "explain[ing] the depth of a Navy Officer's politics." It apparently worked, for there is no evidence that Bankhead's career was in any way affected by his remark.

Paymaster Keeler, who had an uncanny knack for sizing up his commanding officer, greatly admired and respected Bankhead. He once wrote that Bankhead "when satisfied that he was right...did not hesitate to act. If there was anything he abominated and detested it was 'red tape' " "He was a strict disciplinarian exacting obedience and respect from both officers and men....His officers he always expected to do their duty and while they did, were always treated with the greatest courtesy and consideration." And finally, "there was always something about Capt. B. which repelled any attempt at familiarity." Charles A. Post, a young man whose father was a friend of Bankhead, became the captain's clerk on the *Florida*. He agreed with the paymaster's characterization: "Captain Bankhead," he wrote in his diary, "is a splendid fellow and charming companion, though he never forgets that he is captain." Post referred to Bankhead as "his royal highness" in his diary and remarked on his "courtly manners." As Keeler said, Bankhead "while...a model officer...never forgot he was a gentleman."

BIBLIOGRAPHY

The available sources on United States naval officers are relatively rich, especially for the period from the 1840s to the end of the nineteenth century. Nevertheless, both official records and private papers include surprisingly little information about the officers themselves, their physical appearances, political and social philosophies, and their personal lives. There were no "fitness reports" for officers prior to the twentieth century, and rarely do you find a commanding officer informing the Navy Department of the "fitness" of an officer to command. The unfortunate result is that the available information provides more of a chronology of an officer's career than a commentary. This is certainly true of the six officers who commanded the *Monitor*.

The most important single repository for information on the *Monitor* commanders is the National Archives in Washington, D.C. Documents concerning their careers are scattered throughout the various divisions and branches of the Archives. Military, fiscal, coast and geodetic survey, diplomatic, and pension files, to name a few, include information on them. Obviously, the naval records are the most voluminous. Record Group 24 (Bureau of Personnel), and Record Group 45 (Naval Records Collection of the Office of Naval Records and Library) are the most important, although other record groups of naval documents include relevant information. Many of the most important records are available as microfilm publications. They include M330 (abstracts of service of naval officers, 1798-1893); M149 (Letters received by the Secretary of the Navy from Commanders); and M148 (Letters received by the Secretary of the Navy from officers below the rank of commander).

At the Naval Historical Center, Washington Navy Yard, is a group of papers entitled the "ZB File." It includes biographical information on the majority of officers that have served in the navy, including the *Monitor*'s commanders.

There are a number of brief sketches of these officers in various biographical compilations. However, only one such publication, *The National Cyclopedia of American Biography*, includes all six *Monitor* commanders. *The Dictionary of American Biography* includes sketches on all but Bankhead, as does W. N. Powell and Edward Shippen, *Officers of the Army and Navy (Regular) Who Served in the Civil War* (Philadelphia, 1892).

In addition, important material can be found in three published collections of documents and papers relating to the Civil War period: *Official Records of the Union and Confederate Navies in the War of the Rebellion*, 31 vols. (Washington, D.C., 1894-1927); *The War of the Rebellion: A Compilation of the Official Records of the Union and Confederate Armies*, 120 vols. (Washington, D.C., 1880-1901); R. M. Thompson and R. Wainwright (eds.); and *Confidential Correspondence of Gustavus Vasa Fox, Assistant Secretary of the Navy, 1861-1865* 2 vols. (New York, 1918-1919). Finally, the private correspondence of William F. Keeler to his wife is indispensable for the candid and revealing remarks that he made about the six commanding officers. See *Aboard the U.S.S. Monitor, 1862*, Robert W. Daly (ed.) (Annapolis, 1964), and *Aboard the U.S.S. Florida, 1863-1865* (Annapolis, 1968).

For Worden, the biographical sketches include those listed above as well as "John L. Worden" in Clarence E. N. MacCartney, *Mr. Lincoln's Admirals* (New York, 1956); "The Naval Career of Rear Admiral John Lorrimer Worden," *Worden's Past*, IV (October, 1983), 123-127; R. Gerald McMurty, "The Life and Career of John L. Worden," *Lincoln Herald*, LI (October, 1949), 12-30; Clark Reynolds, "John Lorrimer Worden" in *Famous Admirals* (New York, 1987); Lewis R. Hamersly, *Records of Living Officers of the U.S.*

Navy (Philadelphia, 1894); and pension papers for Olivia T. Worden in the National Archives.

Manuscript materials include the Private Papers of John L. Worden, Lincoln Memorial University, Harrogate, Tennessee; the John L. Worden Papers, Naval Historical Foundation, Manuscript Division, Library of Congress; several copies of original correspondence in the "Worden File," Records of the *Monitor* Research and Recovery Foundation, Norfolk, Virginia; and Record Group 78 (Records of the Naval Observatory), National Archives; Record Group 405 (Records of the U.S. Naval Academy), National Archives, particularly entries 10 and 49; M949 (Letters Received by the Superintendent of the U.S. Naval Academy); and a letter from Worden to Mrs. Charlotte Wise Hopkins, March 5, 1888, copy in the *Monitor* National Collection of Artifacts and Papers.

For additional information see Daniel Ammens, *The Old Navy and the New* (Philadelphia, 1898); Park Benjamin, *The United States Naval Academy* (New York, 1900); Frank M. Bennett, *The Steam Navy of the United States* (Pittsburg, 1897); William C. Church, *The Life of John Ericsson* 2 vols. (New York, 1890); George Dewey, *Autobiography of George Dewey, Admiral of the Navy* (New York, 1913); Precival Drayton, *Naval Letters of Captain Percival Drayton, 1861-1865* (New York, 1906); Samuel F. DuPont, *Samuel Francis DuPont: A Selection from his Civil War Letters*, John D. Hayes (ed.) 3 vols., (Ithica, New York, 1969); "First Cruise of the *Montauk*," in *Personal Narratives of Events in the War of the Rebellion*, Rhode Island Soldiers and Sailors Historical Society, Number 1, second series (Providence, 1880); Thomas G. Ford, unpublished history of the United States Naval Academy (copy in the Nimitz Library, Annapolis); Samuel D. Franklin, *Memoirs of a Rear Admiral Who has Served for More than Half a Century in the Navy of the United States* (New York, 1898); Gerald S. Henig, "Admiral Samuel F. DuPont, the Navy Department, and the Attack on Charleston, April 1, 1863," *Naval War College Review,* XXXI (February, 1979), 58-77; Robert E. Johnson, *Rear Admiral John Rogers, 1812-1882* (Annapolis, 1967); James P. Jones, "John L. Worden and the Fort Pickens Mission: The Confederacy's First Prisoner of War," *Alabama Review*, XXI (April, 1968), 113-132; Peter Karsten, *The Naval Aristocracy* (New York, 1972); Dorothy Michelson Livingston, *The Master of Light: A Biography of Albert A. Michelson* (Chicago, 1979); Irving McKee, *Ben-Hur Wallace* (Berkeley, California, 1947); R. Gerald McMurty, "Lincoln's Promotion of John L. Worden," *Lincoln Lore* (1969), 1-3; Robert W. Nesser, "Historical Ships of the Navy: *Montauk.*" *United States Naval Institute Proceedings,* LCVII (May, 1941), 687-691; *Newburgh Daily News* (New York, October 17, 1891), Charles O'Neill, "Engagement Between the *Cumberland* and the *Merrimack*," *United States Naval Institute Proceedings*, XLVIII (June, 1922), 863-893; James R. Soley, *Historical Sketch of the United States Naval Academy* (Washington, D.C., 1876); Charles E. Stedman, *The Civil War Sketchbook of Charles Ellery Stedman, Surgeon, United States Navy* (San Rafael, California, 1976); Jack Sweetman, *U.S. Naval Academy: An Illustrated History* (Annapolis, 1977); Gideon Welles, *The Diary of Gideon Welles, Secretary of the Navy under Lincoln and Johnson*, Howard K. Beale (ed.) 3 vols (New York, 1960).

For Greene, see his private papers in the New York Historical Society, New York City; letters from Worden to F. Pierce, including one concerning Greene in the "Worden File," *Monitor* Research and Recovery Foundation, Norfolk, Virginia; and a copy of a letter from Worden to Secretary of the Navy, June 5, 1868, copy in the "Greene File," *Monitor* Research and Recovery Foundation, Norfolk, Virginia.

See also Concord (New Hampshire) *Evening Monitor*, December 12, 1884; S. Dana Greene, "In the Monitor's Turret," in *Battles and Leaders of the Civil War*, Robert U. Johnson and Clarence C. Buell (eds.) 4 vols. (New York, 1956 edition) 1, 719-729; Greene, "The *Monitor* at Sea and in Battle," *United States Naval Institute Proceedings*, XLIX (November, 1923), 1839-1849; Greene, "I Fired the First Gun and thus Commenced the Great Battle," *American Heritage*, VIII (June, 1957), 102-105; Alfred Thayer Mahan, *The Letters and Papers of Alfred Thayer Mahan*, Robert Seager II and

Dorothy Maguire (eds.) 3 vols (Annapolis, 1975); Seaton Schroeder, *A Half Century of Naval Service* (New York, 1922); Grenville M. Weeks, "The Last Cruise of the Monitor," *Atlantic Monthly*, XI (March, 1863), 366-372.

For Selfridge, there are a number of biographical sketches. In addition to the ones listed previously, they include Eugene Didier, "The Active Rear Admirals of the United States Navy," *Chautauguan*, XXIV (February, 1897), 569-576; Lewis R. Hamersly, *Records of Living Officers of the U.S. Navy* (Philadelphia, 1894); "Thomas O. Selfridge, Jr.," *United Service*, New Series, VII (May, 1892), 529-530; Clark Reynolds, "Thomas O. Selfridge, Jr.," in *Famous Admirals* (New York, 1978).

Selfridge is the only one of the *Monitor* commanders to write his memoirs: *Memoirs of Thomas O. Selfridge, Jr., Rear Admiral, U.S.N.* (New York, 1924). He also wrote several articles: "The *Cumberland*," District of Columbia Commandery, Military order of the Loyal Legion of the United States, *War Papers*, no. 67 (Washington, 1907); "The *Merrimac* and the *Cumberland*," *Cosmopolitan*, XV (June, 1893), 176-184; "The Navy at Fort Fisher," in *Battles and Leaders of the Civil War*, Robert U. Johnson and Clarence C. Buell (eds.) 4 vols (New York, 1956 edition), IV, 362-365. There is also an extensive collection of Selfridge papers in the Naval Historical Foundation, Manuscript Division, Library of Congress.

For additional information on Selfridge, see Edwin C. Bearss, *Hardluck Ironclad: The Sinking and Salvage of the Cairo* (Baton Rouge, 1966); Park Benjamin, *The United States Naval Academy* (New York, 1900); James L. Christley, "The *Alligator*," *Civil War Times Illustrated*, XIX (February, 1981), 26-31; Kenneth J. Hagan, *American Gunboat Diplomacy and the Old Navy 1877-1889* (Westport, Connecticut, 1973); Peter Karsten, *The Naval Aristocracy* (New York, 1972); Clarence E. N. MacCartney, *Mr. Lincoln's Admirals* (New York, 1956); G. Mark, *The Land Divided: A History of the Panama Canal and other Isthmian Canal Projects* (New York, 1944); Sophie P. De Meissner, *Old Naval Days* (New York, 944); John D. Milligan, *Gunboats Down the Mississippi* (Annapolis, 1965); Milton F. Perry, *Infernal Machines: The Story of Confederate Submarine and Mine Warfare* (Baton Rouge, 1965); David D. Porter, *Incidents and Anecdotes of the Civil War* (New York, 1885); Winfield Scott Schley, *Forty-Five Years Under the Flag* (New York, 1904); James R. Soley, *Historical Sketch of the United States Naval Academy* (Washington, D.C., 1876); William N. Still, Jr., *American Sea Power in the Old World* (Westport, Connecticut, 1980); Richard S. West, Jr., *The Second Admiral: A Life of David Dixon Porter, 1813-1819* (New York, 1937).

Jeffers, the fourth commander, has a biographical sketch in the pension papers under his name in the National Archives. See also the ones in the *Dictionary of American Biography* and the *National Cyclopedia of American Biography*.

For additional information, see Park Benjamin, *United States Naval Academy* (New York, 1900); Alexander C. Brown, *Juniper Waterway: A History of the Albemarle and Chesapeake Canal* (Charlottesville, 1981); Rear Admiral Bradley A. Fiske, *From Midshipman to Rear Admiral* (London, 1919); Thomas O. Flickema, "The United States and Paraguay, 1845-1860: Misunderstanding, Miscalculation, and Misconduct," PhD dissertation, Wayne State University, 1965; Samuel R. Franklin, *Memoirs of a Rear Admiral Who Has Served for More than Half a Century in the Navy of the United States* (New York, 1898); Robert E. Johnson, *Rear Admiral John Rodgers, 1812-1882* (Annapolis, 1941-1943); Clare V. McKanna, "The *Water Witch* Incident," *American Neptune*, XXI (January, 1971), 7-18; Vincent Ponko, *Ships, Sea and Scientists: U.S. Naval Exploration and Discovery in the 19th Century* (Annapolis, 1974); Charles L. Price and Claude C. Sturgill, "Shock and Assault in the First Battle of Fort Fisher," *North Carolina Historical Review* XLVII (January, 1970), 24-39; Charles S. Price, unpublished manuscript on the powder boat; Squier, *Notes on Central America. . .and the Proposed Honduras Inter-Oceanic Railway* (New York, 1971 reprint); Harris G. Warren, *Paraguay: An Informal History* (Norman Oklahoma); Charles Wilkes, *Autobiography of Rear Admiral Charles Wilkes, U.S. Navy 1798-1877*, William James Morgan, et.al. (eds.)

(Washington, D.C., 1978); John H. Williams, *The Rise and Fall of the Paraguayan Republic 1800-1876* (Austin, 1979).

There are a number of biographical sketches of Stevens. See especially the one in the *Dictonary of American Biography;* Lewis R. Hamersly, *Records of Living Officers of the U.S. Navy* (Philadelphia, 1894); and Hamersly, *Biographical Sketches of Distinguished Officers of the Army and Navy* (New York, 1905); Charlotte M. Conger, "Rear Admiral Thomas H. Stevens, USN," *United Service*, New Series, XV (June, 1896), 565-570; "T. H. Stevens, USN," *United Service*, New Series, V (May, 1891), 545-548. The Duke University Manuscript Division has a collection of private Stevens papers, as does the Naval Historical Foundation, Manuscript Divison, Library of Congress. Finally, a small but important collection of Stevens letters, including one describing the battle of Mobile Bay, is in private possession.

See also Daniel Ammen, *The Old Navy and the New* (Philadelphia, 1891); Stuart L. Bernath, *Squall Across the Atlantic: American Civil War Prize Cases and Diplomacy* (Berkeley, 1970); Joseph C. Bruzek, "The U.S. Schooner Yacht *America*," *United States Naval Institute Proceedings*, XCIII (September, 1967), 1159-1187; William W. Davis, *The Civil War and Reconstruction in Florida* (Gainesville, 1964 reprint); Charles H. Jenrich, "Schooner *America*: Mistress of Many," *Boating Magazine* (September, 1974), 41, 84-86; John E. Johns, *Florida During the Civil War* (Gainesville, 1964); Peter Karsten, *The Naval Aristocracy* (New York, 1972); Charles Lewis, David Glasgow Farragut 2 vols. (Annapolis, 1941-1943); Clarence E. N. MacCartney, *Mr. Lincoln's Admiral* (New York, 1956); Alfred Thayer Mahan, *The Letters and Papers of Alfred Thayer Mahan*, Robert Seager, II, and Dorothy Maguire (eds.) 3 vols (Annapolis, 1975); Thomas R. Neblett, "The Yacht *America*: A New Acount Pertaining to her Confederate Operations." *American Neptune* XXVII (October, 1967), 233-253; Frank L. Owsley, Jr., *The C.S.S. Florida: Her Building and Operations* (Philadelphia, 1965); Charles Ellery Stedman, *The Civil War Sketchbook of Charles Ellery Stedman, Surgeon, United States Navy* (San Rafael, California, 1976); Charles Wilkes, *Autobiography of Rear Admiral Charles Wilkes, U.S. Navy 1798-1877*, William James Morgan, et. al. (eds.) (Washington, D.C., 1978).

Bankhead is the least written about of all the *Monitor* commanders, probably because he died shortly after the war ended. The only known sketches are in the *National Cyclopedia of American Biography* and J. E. Warren, "The Bankhead Family," *William and Mary Quarterly* IX (October, 1919), 303-314.

See also Charles D. Chadbourn, III, "Sailor and Diplomat: U.S. Naval Operations in China, 1865-1877," PhD Dissertation, University of Washington, 1976; Salmon P. Chase, *Inside Lincoln's Cabinet: The Civil War Diary of Salmon P. Chase*, David Donald (ed.) (New York, 1954); Samuel F. DuPont, *Samuel Francis DuPont: A Selection from His Civil War Letters*, John D. Hayes (ed.) 3 vols (Ithica, New York, 1969); Robert E. Johnson, *Far China Station: The U.S. Navy in Asian Waters 1800-1898* (Annapolis, 1979); Edgar S. McClay, *Reminiscences of the Old Navy* (New York, 1898); Military Essays and Recollections, Illinois Commandery Loyal Legion of the United States (Chicago, 1891); Milton F. Perry, *Infernal Machines: The Story of Confederate Submarine and Mine Warfare* (Baton Rouge, 1965); Charles A. Post, "A Diary on the Blockade in 1863," *United States Naval Institute Proceedings*, XLIV (October-November, 1918), 2333-2350; Craig Symonds (ed.), *Charleston Blockade: The Journal of John P. Marchand, USN* (Newport, Rhode Island, 1976); Grenville M. Weeks, "The Last Cruise of the *Monitor*," *Atlantic Monthly*, XI (March, 1863), 266-372; Gideon Welles, *The Diary of Gideon Welles, Secretary of the Navy under Lincoln and Johnson*, Howard K. Beale (ed.) 3 vols. (New York, 1960).

Finally, a number of general works provided essential background information. For the navy during the nineteenth century, the best single work is E. B. Potter and Chester W. Nimitz, *Sea Power: A Naval History* (Englewood Cliffs, New Jersey, 1960). Bern Anderson's *By Sea and By River* (New York, 1962) is still the best study of the naval history of the Civil War, although it lacks balance. For the *Monitor*, the best study is Edward M. Miller, *U.S.S. Monitor: The Ship That Launched a Modern Navy* (Annapolis, 1978). While a midshipman at the Naval Academy, Miller edited a work entitled *Project Cheesebox: A Journey into History* 3 vols. (Annapolis, 1974). William C. Davis, *Duel Between the First Ironclads* (Garden City, New York, 1975), is also a good account of the *Monitor* as well as her opponent at Hampton Roads. For the battle in Hampton Roads, see also William N. Still, Jr., *Iron Afloat: The Story of the Confederate Armorclads*. For an analysis of the Union monitors, see Still, "The New Ironclads," in *Guns of '62 (Garden City, 1981)*.

www.ingramcontent.com/pod-product-compliance
Lightning Source LLC
Chambersburg PA
CBHW080524110426
42742CB00017B/3227